THE HIDDEN POWER OF YOUR SUBCONSCIOUS MIND

How to program your deepest
part and improve yourself

CONTENTS

Introduction to psychology

Psychology is the scientific investigation of how behavior, cognition, and emotion.

Psych is an academic and implemented field between the study of mental processes and behavior. Psychology additionally indicates the effective use of such knowledge to different spheres of individual actions, for example, about humans' everyday lives and the cure of mental disease.

Psychology is different from another societal science -- anthropology, economics, political science, and sociology -- at that psych attempts to spell out the mental processes and behavior of both men and women. Where-as research and neuroscience analyze that the neural or biological procedures along with how they relate to the psychological ramifications they subjectively generate, psych is generally involved about the interaction of mental processes and behavior onto the systemic stage. Even the sub-field of all neuro-psychology studies that specific neural procedures even though biological psych studies that the biological foundations of practice and mental conditions.

Psych is an academic and applied field involving the analysis of behavior, mind, and idea and also the sub-conscious neural foundations of behavior. Psychology additionally indicates the effective use of such knowledge to different spheres of human activity, including problems of individuals' everyday lives and the cure of mental disease. It's concerned with humans, although the behavior and mental processes of creatures may likewise be a portion of psych exploration, just as an issue in its own appropriate (e.g., animal cognition and ethology), or somewhat more controversially, as a style of getting an insight into human psychology with contrast (like relative psych). Psychology is usually described as the science of behavior and mental methods.

Psychology does not reference the brain, or the nervous system also will be framed purely regarding phenomenological or information processing theories of mind. Significantly, however, a better comprehension of brain function is being included in psychological theory and exercise, especially in parts like artificial intelligence, neuro psychology, along with cognitive neuroscience.

Psychology clarifies and efforts to spell out awareness, behavior, and societal interaction. Experimental psych is mostly committed to describing human action and reaction since it genuinely does occur. Back in the last twenty decades or so, psych has started to inspect the relationship between the brain or nervous system. It's not clear in exactly what ways those socialize: does understanding figure out brain countries or perform brain countries find comprehension - or even so are going in a variety of manners: possibly to comprehend that you want to be familiar with the significance of "consciousness" and also "brain condition" - or will be understanding some form of challenging 'illusion' which conveys no direct relationship to neural procedures? The late 19th century marks the beginning of psychology as a scientific venture. The last year 1879, is commonly regarded as the beginning of psychology as an unaffiliated area of analysis, as in that year, German scientist Wilhelm Wundt established the very first laboratory dedicated exclusively to psychological research in Leipzig, Germany.

Wundt mixed philosophical introspection with methods and lab apparatuses caused by his bodily reports with Helmholtz, in addition to a number of the or her style and design. This experimental introspection was compared from that which had already been predicted psychology before afterward, a branch of doctrine whereby men and women introspected on their own.

Early devices of behavior

Wundt's type of psych would be referred to as structuralism. It's genuinely a category called orderly interpretations as it strove to spell out each behavior together about an orderly stance. Other approaches to psych are functionalism, behaviorism, gestalt psych, and psycho-dynamic psych.

Functionalism is worried regarding all the rationale behind behavior rather than the structure of this brain. It enabled the research of fresh themes, for example, kids and creatures.

Behaviorism is a way of psychology. Depending on the proposal, that behavior could also be researched clarified clinically with no recourse to both inner mental conditions. Psychologists who use behaviorism are worried chiefly with muscle motions and glandular secretions.

Gestalt psych can be a concept of mind and brain, which suggests the basic functional principle of this brain is more holistic, parallel, and even mind-boggling, together with self-organizing trends. It's a particular fascination with perceptual problems and the way they are sometimes translated. Even a gestalt considers the entire is far more than different than the total amount of each one the areas. Attempting to split behavior into different pieces is simplistic as everything changes anything.

Sigmund Freud initially practiced psycho-dynamic psych, but he did not plan this to function as a technique.

Perspectives

Even though the usage of 1 method to address the majority of psychologists left all of the problems, these ancient systems were critical at the evolution of new approaches and thoughts. You can find just eight prominent viewpoints that psychologists commonly take, but a lot of utilize the various technique rather than limiting themselves into one.

The psycho-dynamic view emphasizes subconscious drives along with the settlement of battles, the behavioral highlights that the purchase and adjustment of visible reactions, and also the humanistic ways make an effort to attain optimum human capacity set in Maslow's hierarchy of desires.

The biological view is that the scientific research of this organic foundation of behavior and mental conditions are incredibly closely associated with neuroscience.

Evolutionary psych is a theoretical solution to psychology which attempts to describe specified mental and mental faculties --like memory, understanding, or speech since improved adaptations, i.e., while the operational services and products of the usual or sexual variety.

Cognitive psych takes using this clear strategy; however, it rejects introspection as a valid system of analysis. It needs to be mentioned that Herbert Simon and Allen Newell determined that the thinking-aloud' protocol," by which researchers view an issue, participated in introspection, also that talks his thoughts, therefore enabling analysis of their meditation.

Societal psych could be your study of how men and women's feelings, emotions, and behaviors are affected by the actual, imagined, or implied presence of many others (Allport, 1985).

Wundt contended that "we understand a bit concerning our minds in relaxed, random self-observation. Observations must be created with educated observers below strictly defined terms to reply to a well-defined query. "

Lots of boffins withdrew off the thought of how introspection as a portion of psych since the monitoring of stimulation was insecure with no philosophical strategy.

No matter how true and contrary to introspection referred to as extrospection was established with compared to psychophysics. Psychophysics is your division of psychology, managing the relationship between physical stimuli and their understanding.

The major difference is that Wundt took this process into the experimental stadium and so into the freshly organized emotional niche. Other significant early contributors to the business of psych include Hermann Ebbinghaus (a pioneer in studies on memory), the Russian Ivan Pavlov (who discovered the learning process of classical conditioning), and also the Austrian Sigmund Freud.

Even the mid-20th century witnessed a rejection of Freud's theories among many psychologists as being too unscientific, in addition being a reaction against Edward Titchener's abstract approach to the mind.

Edward b. Titchener (1876-1927) has been an Englishman as well as also a scholar of Wilhelm Wundt ahead of eventually become a professor of psychology at Cornell college. He'd put their spin on Wundt's psychology of awareness afterward he emigrated into the U.S.

At the beginning of the 19thcentury that the heritage daddy of experimental psych Wilhelm Wundt strove to experimentally validate his theory, which conscious mental lifestyle might be separated into fundamental parts that subsequently sort more technical spiritual buildings. Wundt's structuralism was immediately abandoned since it couldn't be able to be analyzed in an identical way like behavior, prior to date, whenever the brain-scanning technological innovation could differentiate, as an instance, specialized brain cells which respond solely to fundamental shapes and lines and how are subsequently united into succeeding brain areas at which increasingly more technical visual buildings have been shaped. The distinct research from science is named cognitive psych as opposed to structuralism due to the fact Wundt's period never stopped to become connected to all the problem of observability.

Most science fiction is predicated on the framework derived from cognitive psychology, even though the prevalence of the paradigm doesn't exclude the others, that can be frequently implemented as needed. Psychologists devoted to some specific locations, nevertheless, could make use of the cognitive psych just infrequently in any respect.

Cognitive psych maybe your psychological science that studies cognition, the mental processes which can be shown to underlie behavior. This handles a wide selection of research domains, examining questions about the workings of memory, awareness, understanding, knowledge representation, reasoning imagination, and problem fixing.

Chapter one

The power (potential) within you

Three emotional truth that could boost your inner power

A few of us will reach fantastic issues. The others won't. However, is this? All of us are only "chatting monkeys onto a natural space ship flying throughout the world," since joe Rogan sets it. Therefore, why would a few "talking monkeys" assemble 8 or 7 figure organizations, traveling the earth, and are living the life span in their fantasies as the others folks... Appropriately, the desire we're living the life span of their imaginations.

What is the gap between these and us? The fantastic thing isn't just a complete lot. You're equally as competent because they're. You're equally as powerful and filled with possibility since they're. They only know that a couple of things concerning hacking on their psych and unlocking their internal power you most likely do not understand.

Here are three emotional details that may unleash your inner power:

1. Your ideas just determine the best way to believe

Through the majority of the 1900s, psychologists used behavioral treatment to successfully treat individuals who have anxiety, depressive disorders, eating problems, dependency, you identify it. All of us form of guessing, if you would like to adjust some body's activities, then you want to modify their activities!

It was around 1960 that Albert Ellis indicated the proven revolutionary fact concerning our profoundly held beliefs regarding the entire world (i.e., how we presume), precisely what he named our "fundamental snobby assumptions,"" ascertain the way we believe and ergo, the way we act. It was subsequently implied that if you would like to alter your activities or behaviors, you need first to change the direction that you imagine.

Today, a whole division of psych, chased cognitive treatment, is specialized in this assumption. And that the consequences are somewhat shocking; drugs together with behavioral and cognitive therapy are currently 75 percent to 90 percent more effective. To put it differently, if you would like to improve how you act and the way you feel, then subsequently alter the direction that you believe. Much easier said previously, " I understand. Continue reading.

2. Your mind can not inform the gap between reality and imagination

Perhaps you have thought about something humorous that occurred after which captured your self-laughing or grinning at people? You've! Almost all of us have. However, is this? After all, the humorous issue happened -- therefore, why have you been talking about any of it at the moment? Properly, it is because the mind cannot tell the gap between reality and imagination.

In the event you envision a great thing occurring, then you'll encounter each of the beneficial emotions that you connect with this fantastic item as though it transpired. The same goes for unwanted encounters. That is this kind of revolutionary emotional actuality that one particular analysis demonstrated there isn't a lot of gap between picturing moving into the gymnasium and visiting the fitness center!

Therefore, how is this essential? It signifies that, using just a small amount of how intentionality, you can reposition the human brain to connect pleasure or pain with all these activities you pick. By picturing the near future consequences of one's lousy behaviors and also the long-term advantages of desirable behaviors, you're able to attest real enthusiasm to improve and also accept the very first faltering step in developing a new life which arouses you.

3. You are better in creating a brand fresh custom when you're currently ceasing a terrible routine

You can't ever give up a terrible routine, maybe you are not ready, at least. The custom pathway on your brain is formed, and there is no known solution just to infect that pathway entirely. However, you may transform the path. You may set a brand-new behavior within the habitual trigger-behavior-reward program. Charles Duhigg, " the author of the power of routine phone calls this "the golden principle of practice, adjust: "you cannot instill an unfortunate habit, so you may just change it out."

This is the reason why individuals who are making effort to stop smoking, chew gum, and take alcoholics beverage caffeinated drinks -- as those things are substitutes to your terrible routine.

In a situation where you want to stop a particular habit such as overeating, oversleeping, smoking, drinking, etc. Don't make attempt to stop, consider starting something new to replace the old habit. Frequently, contemplating ending only leaves, you would like to participate together with the terrible addiction more as you are considering any of it! However, exchange the terrible dependence using something both gratifying, something fantastic for you, and you're going to have the ability to improve any unwanted behavior immediately.

How can you specify interior power?

Inner power could be your silent pressure within one who understands when to behave when to proceed and grants you the energy to achieve that.

Have you read about the story about a mother who lifted up an automobile with her bare hands to save her child that was trapped beneath? If that's the period of death or life, she tapped to her internal power. Someone could feel overly tried to walk or move, however should somebody shout fire! He finds out the energy to perform.

This inner power is something most of us possess. However, we will need to master to tap it into imaginative and compelling methods within our day-to-day lifespan.

Now you climbed in the humblest of beginnings to accomplish expert power. What do you know concerning endurance?

To begin with, without having god, I'd not be right here now. What else would a small lady from the small village at Korea that was simply tagged a curse along with evil fortune grow up to turn into high-tech CEO, writer, motivational speaker, and much more?

Achieving my goals failed to arrive immediately. Step-by-step, i had to produce the requirements that could let me actualize my dreams.

To split from this box, individuals were attempting to help keep me trapped inside, " I needed to pick each day maybe not to permit hard predicaments to overpower me.

My first job when I came to the U.S Was cleaning baths in a lodge. People called me a lot of dreadful names. I always needed to validate: "they're not my god. I was of who and exactly what I am. I understood exactly the way that led me there".

These struggles, " I heard an essential lesson: even though we could sense as though the barriers we confront are insurmountable, that is perhaps not correct. We have to continue to the fantasies and maintain performing our role as the upcoming massive breakthrough is waiting to input our own lives in only the most suitable minute.

Just as an urge for women's power, what you presume females most want to attain power?

On reach power, ladies want absolute and total honesty. When ladies might be frank and take their flaws in addition to their strengths, doorways of liberty and opportunity will probably open to them. Whenever you make up your mind and face a weakness, then you consistently benefit an increment of power as you're carrying the very first measure to grow.

Honesty also means, not exactly what someone expects you to become. Tapping into your internal power to remain faithful to a yourself can be the origin of everything I instruct: you're just one of some sorts. A daisy certainly not inquires itself, "why are not I personally an improved?" each portion of production, for example, you, has its beauty and also its strength

Precisely what may be the one most essential point to understand about every one of these methods above to interior power?

Even the seven measures to interior power are joining along the human entire body and mind as you can so that your thinking and activities are tasked accountable for one's own goals; detecting the facts yourself; attaining strength of human body-mind, and soul therefore that you may convey your authentic disposition; learning how to love yourself; preserving devotion for your targets and lifestyle; learning how to forfeit unnecessary and flaws pursuits and attachments therefore that you may accomplish your aims; and also trying patience at all that you need to do.

Even the most crucial point to learn concerning these ways above is which you simply can't perform you measure minus others should you genuinely want to split into fantastic. Every one of the steps come with each other to attract wholeness for your becoming.

Perhaps not every one of the hurdles people confront originates out of. What interior limits do persons, as well as maybe notably ladies, placed forth by themselves?

Most folks possess an interior conversation that states, "I am not adequate" or even "i really don't deserve it" or also "i don't have what it takes" this usually stems in several years of listening in to all other people's viewpoints folks overcritical moms and dads, covetous colleagues, aggressive allies, along with also others.

When we purchase inside that misinformation, we eventually become our own worst enemies. We usually do not cure ourselves nicely. If a person else handled you together with hate, criticism, or disrespect, then you'd not endure this. Therefore, what exactly makes it right that you treat yourself which manner?

Stop terrorizing yourself! It is the right time for you to alter your inner dialogue and understand and tune in and link up with your inner self (your authentic, initial self-explanatory and interior voice) that claims that you simply have all of the power you want to meet your fantasies.

All of us live in a civilized world where kids are taught to be afraid of making mistakes. Do you believe this is a smart path?

No! Once you make a mistake, then this indicates you're doing something. Is not this lovely? In the event you don't conduct anything, then you won't create errors, yet nevertheless, you won't receive outcomes, and you're going to go nowhere.

" I do not consider mistakes as something that is unwanted. I admit my response was not exactly what I required, therefore that i got to shift, explore longer, and also be much creative. I educate my pupils to study faults. Just as an issue of simple fact, I state: create an incredible blunder!

The best way many errors did alexander graham bell create when devising calling? Exactly how many blunders did engineers create even though acquiring the cell-phone?

Who disagrees? The goal is always to triumph and not rely on your own mistakes. That is the reason my motto is "They could do, she could perform, you will want to me."

Who'd benefit from studying your publication?

Anybody can gain knowledge through your publication. I wrote this paper it if you hunger for lifetime, encounter troubles, and try for victory and also enjoyment. Who does not suffer from problems or struggles within their lifetime? Almost all of us do.

"I share precisely what I heard in early fighting styles convention together side years of my very own real-world adventure helping men and women remain on target and meet their visions and aims, and also know to continue to keep their power on-- irrespective of what struggles they're confronting.

In case you'd just one part of the information, what could it not be and for that?

This is for anybody with a vision, fantasy, or aim (do not confuse goals and targets together with day-dreams and dreams): there's just you. Study your thumbprint. It's exceptional.

Thus, keep in mind that it is their own life! Nobody could eat food for you, sleep for you, or take a piss for you. In a situation where you don't like what you see, you can decide immediately to improve the photograph of one's own life. You're in charge of that which you're doing to your creative energy inside this second

The way your truth about your-self limit your prospective

Right at this time, you're talking about yourself. Every day you speak about the entire world around you-- deciphering, stressing. What's more, you talk with your self-concerning your personal life.

Determined by upon your own beliefs on your own as well as your environment, your self-talk can allow you to accomplish emotional wellbeing and professional and personal victories, or it may cause you to get depressed and severely restrict your capability to develop healthy relationships and also detect joy in your life.

Most of your subconscious beliefs grown throughout your youth.

Just as a youngster, you soaked your environment up and forced significance from what you watched, learned, and so we're also told. If every single time you have made your mum delivered one into an own room with dinner, then you first heard more than spoiling your rage. In case your dad merely paid out care for your requirements personally when you brought home decorations, profitably grew to become the one thing which bothers for your needs personally.

sometimes, your beliefs shielded you personally and assisted you to browse through you life. However, as a grownup, presuming that you can't ever say your rage that winning is all that things - will not enable you. It restricts you.

On comprehend the way your subconscious beliefs impression your own life, consider these as though they indeed are a portion of the mathematical formula.

Even the American psychologist Albert Ellis (1913-2007) suggested an exact straightforward formulation to spell out the precisely complicated manners we answer environment: a + bc.

Even a stand for "activating celebration": you now own friends project because in just two weeks and most of your downline has gone home early. Your lovely date called you to get a next.

B stands for "perception": people usually make the most out of my workout. There's something fundamentally wrong with me. I am unlovable.

C stands for "consequence": you end the job all on your own and see the much bitterness on your colleagues, then they don't encourage one with the media lunches. Rather than choosing the initiative to telephone and also have out them yourself, you put in their name into a vast collection of all individuals who are bothering you.

Today that you understand the utmost level to that your faith about your self induces your behavior, you could observe changing them is vitally essential. To do so, you want to find and procedure that the defective believing supporting them—releasing unwanted energies and substituting it by new beliefs which encourage your wellbeing.

Just as the expression goes, people that do not learn from history are doomed to repeat their mistakes. In the event you may be aware of someone's past, then you may opt never to replicate older, restricting behaviors. Afterward, you definitely may view an issue from a new point of view --a newcomer's mind that lets you produce new decisions that could boost your life.

On realizing your subconscious view, the next time you get angry, take your time to listen to self-talk utilizing mindfulness. Sit quietly using all the emotion and genuinely let yourself have it.

Where does one believe it on the human physique? What idea does this cause?

Socialize for things such as:

• I cannot be pleased until all is ideal, and that I never fail to neglect in making matters flawless.

• my entire life is as if it is turning out of hands; I want to get ready for the worst.

• I am aware of the conditions of my own experience that might shift; it'd mend how exactly I feel indoors.

Once you've recognized the impression that is tripping your emotion...

Ask these questions:

• what's the source?

• can it support me?

• can it hold me?

• can it induce me to use it in the place of dread?

• could i exchange it having an even productive impression?

This procedure was motivated by Douglas Lanier's post in psych nowadays, could someone change your disposition.

Measure 1: feeling of somebody who you respect or envy. Produce a set of attributes or qualities which your compliance or worry concerning these. Choose anyone to focus on.

Measure 2: picture what it'd seem like should you uttered that caliber at the moment on work, relationships, and emotional processes.

Measure 3: ascertain on your journal, how exactly foolish this caliber might change your life. If, as an instance, you are using the ability of persistence, you will respect in somebody, just how your life may alter whenever you recover the power.

Measure 4: brainstorm a record of things that you can do daily to fortify this measurement of yourself just as you are strengthening a muscle building.

Measure 5: ultimately, "behave like" become you presently own this caliber, as though it truly is previously an essential component of you personally. Since David Richo writes, "initially what this means behaving like' but we behave together, and more of those concealed powers eventually become us."

Through your effort, elegance should soon come. By way of this mindful process, you also will wind up becoming more of yourself every day.

Chapter two

How your mind works

The way to comprehend the mind

Our brains do a lot of things that are coping using you may become a puzzling jumble. How frequently have you ever experienced blended notions, emotions, thoughts, remedies, and also memories peeled for a few mental real estates, while looking to keep dedicated to somebody different?

Cognitive critics have attempted to make sense of it while using them for several decades. However, a lot of the outcome signal has been faked. But in the last twenty decades, a significant motif surfaced that has been a breakthrough," that is not something brand new to ordinary psychologists of nowadays.

Even the key discovery shows that our brains performs in two procedures: people who operate mechanically (usually called technique 1) and also the ones which are somewhat more effortful (procedure 2). The

Length of mind

To get the descriptions beneath to earn feel, " I ask one to believe about an extreme case for all in the life. You may have used three at the last handful of moments looking over this informative article. After getting aware of these, they really should care far more evident and straightforward to operate together with. I'll even give a good example of all that happened to me while hanging outside, having a close friend.

1. Engaged mind

This is the condition to be immersed in or associated with, that which we have been doing from the current second. After we're fully within a dialogue, ski down a hill, screaming right after hearing a buddy having lunch, or even carrying the very first snack of this optimal piece of pizza on earth; ostensibly, if our ideas and care are wholly associated to precisely what is happening here and now, that's participated mind.

2. Automated mind

Our brain is continuously running a vast scope of activities. For example,, we know some shifts in the natural environment (fresh noises, alterations in lighting or fever, speedy motions, etc.) And some other distress or physiological senses that have to get detected (plus a number which do not). We make decisions and evaluations been a breakthrough," that is not something brand new to ordinary psychologists of nowadays.

Even the key discovery shows that our brains performs in two procedures: people who operate mechanically (usually called technique 1) and also the ones which are somewhat more effortful (procedure 2). The

Length of mind

To get the descriptions beneath to earn feel, " I ask one to believe about an extreme case for all in the life. You may have used three at the last handful of moments looking over this informative article. After getting aware of these, they really should care far more evident and straightforward to operate together with. I'll even give a good example of all that happened to me while hanging outside, having a close friend.

1. Engaged mind

This is the condition to be immersed in or associated with, that which we have been doing from the current second. After we're fully within a dialogue, ski down a hill, screaming right after hearing a buddy having lunch, or even carrying the very first snack of this optimal piece of pizza on earth; ostensibly, if our ideas and care are wholly associated to precisely what is happening here and now, that's participated mind.

2. Automated mind

Our brain is continuously running a vast scope of activities. For example,, we know some shifts in the natural environment (fresh noises, alterations in lighting or fever, speedy motions, etc.) And some other distress or physiological senses that have to get detected (plus a number which do not). We make decisions and evaluations concerning matters being negative or positive (which includes ourselves), categorize our adventures, and also create arrangements regarding things that we will need to do along with the need to be mindful. We've got scenes out of our earlier sparked and possess beliefs and feelings relating to matters which may occur later on. We shape customs to automate significant sections of their own lives and also, therefore, are pulled outside of minutes together with questions or memories. This nonstop stream of advice a part of becoming individual, and also, we spend quite a big time of their own lives swimming within this flow. That is an automated mind.

3. Analytic mind

Since we're self-indulgent critters, we can deliberately measure straight back from our real feelings, emotions, and adventures to better detect them, manipulate data inside our minds, and also clear up problems. Each one of the intricate justifications we can perform would be everything I predict in the analytical account.

You will find out that all those diverse manners, analytical mind will operate, and I have six broad types beneath. Also, lots of the ideas processes take go through the analytical mind. The gap here is the fact that a systematic account is if people blatantly opt to use those talents.

Watch: we could detect different men and women, in addition to the joys of their minds.

Mirror: we can unleash events from our thoughts and arrive in a new point of view.

Post: we may carry instantaneous matters and problems to seek out remedies or comprehension.

Prepare: we can organize profoundly in the long run and make backup alternatives.

Concentrate: we could keep the focus on something essential.

Envision: we may use our imaginations to run through just how something may work.

Assessing the mind

There certainly are a couple of standard manners. I feel those "frames of mind" are utilized to enhance our own lives. To begin with, I believe this breakdown helps us know different purposes our own mind and also could help us better in developing a better understanding of which framework we might desire to be at any particular time. As an instance, whenever there was some exciting or crucial going about, we have to participate. When there's a complicated problem available, we ought to assess it.

How our mind work

Research shows that "if someone is pondering knowingly (as recorded by eeg gear) after which targets on a single naturally occurrence like noise, a visual feeling, or an image, the brain waves keep on being ostensibly precise the same and notions persist stream throughout the mind. We can increase our mind's awareness of comprising just one perceptual input but keep believing knowingly without tripping our focus on our notions. But whenever the mind focuses on two sensory information in an identical period (a solid along with also an image, for example, or breath and pulse), all of the notions nearly instantaneously stops going through the mind.

Mental designs

Mental routine is a memory hint shaped on your brain tissue to capture anything you've observed. Anything you see, listen to, sense, smell, taste, or sense something repeatedly, your brain assembles a blueprint for it.

If you encounter it, or something similar, the human brain activates the existent memory hint or patterned believing, and you move on autopilot.

Capacity our running performance

The largest possible number of things we could save in our working-memory, or in our conscious mind, is four or three. In the event, you have to put up many more goods in the mind at the same time. Use tricks such as copying items above repeatedly, or group goods with each other, such as people do using phone amounts.

Intelligence relates to memory foam - that's the further advice you may take in mind at the same time. The more info you may inter-relate. For those who have a higher functioning memory that is → creative problem-solving skills tend to be higher.

Mediation

Meditation has become the most powerful mind instrument developed. Meditation was clinically demonstrated to enhance → imagination, intellect, memory, and endurance, and also to incorporate abandoned and right brain work out. It's been shown to improve bodily, mental, and emotional wellness

1-3 strategies to begin training your sub-conscious mind to find exactly what you would like

Your brain is made to fortify and modulate your own life.

Your subconscious mind has something known as a homeostatic urge that modulates works such as human body temperature, breathing, and heartbeat. Brian Tracy discussed it similar to that: "during your nervous program, [your homeostatic impulse] keeps a balance on the list of countless of compounds on your countless cells that your full physical system works at full stability the majority of the time."

However, what a lot of people don't know is the fact that as the brain is produced to modulate yours itself, so does it strive to increase your mental self. The mind is constantly composing and sending to your awareness info and stimulation, which supports your own pre-existing beliefs (that is called psychology like affirmation prejudice) in addition to connecting you with all recurrent notions and instincts which mimic and also reflect which you have achieved previously.

Your subconscious mind could be your gatekeeper of one's relaxation zone.

Additionally, it can also be the kingdom in that you may habituate to expect and also frequently search the activities that could construct and fortify, the best victory, enjoyment, wholeness, or curative of one's own life.

1. Be eager to observe the inevitable shift.

Even the first measure into creating a massive shift in your life doesn't think it is potential; it is getting ready to see if it's likely.

Now you are going to leap out of really being truly a comprehensive skeptic into some parasite that is overburdened. The measure between people will be only being offered to watch precisely what is potential. You may try out sending some "frightful mails," by that you merely propose a customer or companion to get something which they usually do not have any excuse to react to. You may have a couple of dozen messages that are discounted, but someone will respond.

Even the purpose is you are eager to view whether it's likely... That is what's going to affect your own life.

2. Give your self-permission to become more prosperous.

As an alternative of precisely the exact kind of the story of presuming you will end up joyful once you are ten lbs. one promotion and also two-lifetime occurrences down the-line, focus with changing up your interior monologue into: "I enable my entire life to become good."

3. Never let different people's anxieties to throw shadows of uncertainty.

Even the way people give information of one's victory will say the way they're doing within their own lives.

In case you declare your participation, those that have been in joyful marriages will probably be happy for you. Individuals who come in miserable marriages will tell you also. It is tight, and you need to love your staying period since "only" men and women.

Even the point is the others' anxieties are projections in the very own circumstances. They don't have anything regarding whatever you're are not capable of.

4. Familiarizing yourself with sound reinforcement.

Maintain a glass of champagne in the icebox. Alter your early morning alert in your mobile to read through the following information: "congratulations!!!" make sure the things which you touch and see many often bring-you pleasure and also hopefulness. Maintain a motivational mentality and be conscious over a post-it close on your pc. Stop following people make you feel terrible about yourself and stick to people that find themselves always post inspirational messages along with intriguing thoughts. Create your news-feed an area that may catalyze your growth, rather than decreasing your understanding of one's values.

5. Discuss your good results as a real simple fact, perhaps not an upcoming program.

Even though you must not say things such as "I generate a semi," or also "I am a CEO," should they aren't in reality, don't begin talking by precisely what it is which you would like from living maybe not at the context you are one day chase it, however, you will be living.

As an alternative of saying: "I expect to achieve this one day" state, "I'm unashamed of the way to do that today." in the place of believing, "I am glad if I'm at another place within my life," presume, "I'm capable of being joyful here, and at the moment, nothing at all is keeping me."

6. Produce a fantasy distance.

Fully being able to envision what exactly it is that you would like in your life will be utterly critical for generating because if you don't understand where you are moving, then you won't understand how to reverse.

Once you now own a superior image from the mind for precisely what exactly it is which you need and the way that it is which you would like to live your life, you're capable of starting to reevaluate and actualize it. If you're still ripped or discriminated between that which you would like, you are going to be left not capable of carrying authentic, purposeful actions supporting whatever.

Whether or not you employ a Pinterest plank blog, site, laptop, or plank, set up images and words that reflect exactly what you would like and the way you would like to call home.

7. Describe your immunity.

When our subconscious minds get us back again from chasing our fantasies, it is because we're carrying a contradictory view concerning any of it.

Identify your immunity and question yourself. Ask yourself the reason why you truly feel a lot better once you procrastinate or getting precisely what you want might set you in an area that causes you to feel much more susceptible than you felt before.

Locate a means to fulfill those demands until you move.

8. Take a master's policy for your own life.

Forget five or maybe ten years Ideas; thus far varies within the years it truly is precisely not possible to establish aims you'll be in a position to maintain. Most importantly, time after time, much far better chances will present itself, although your life won't look as if you assumed it'd, you are far better off because of it.

Alternatively, have a grasp program. Describe your core values and motives. Request precisely what would be your best objective of things you would like to reach as you're living; picture the type of heritage that you would like to let go of. Once you've got your enormous picture worth recorded, you'll make decisions to your long-term, which aligns with yourself.

9. Begin a gratitude journal.

Even the finest solution to begin putting yourself at a head-space of "with" instead of "needing" would always be to commence a gratitude clinic. By being thankful for everything you have you, you alter your mindset against being famished because of shift into atmosphere fulfilled with exactly where you're in. Nothing magnetizes prosperity for your requirements, enjoy gratitude. There exists an expression that as soon as you think you've plenty of, you're receptive to obtaining increasingly more and increasingly a lot more. That's correct.

Start asking for everything you would like, even if you recognize you are going to be refused.

In case someone requests one to accomplish a consulting undertaking, request for a payment you wish to have for the service. In case you aim to get promoted in the company where you work, then sit with your high upward and also make your goals understood—touch base to brand names that you wish to get the job done together with. Start seeking whatever you would like, even when you don't have a motive to feel that anybody will provide you with some of these matters. Finally, they are going to.

1-1. Publish your attachment into this" how."

Your job would be to spot the things, after which to get the job done in conjunction with different men and women in the best possible way.

In case you would aim to do the job liberally and conduct your company, rather than quitting in case your very first effort fails, then consider re-imagining how else you might reach your goal in a brand new way which is a lot more monetarily prosperous.

Even the point is the fact that life will surprise you with how matters appear to fruition—rather than being sporadically connected with every tiny detail working out how you imagine that it needs to be amenable to possibility and potential. Also, support is anything that you have never envisioned previously.

1-2. Familiarizing yourself.

Start spending time together with people that are thorough, creative, and supportive.

In case you are chilling out just about every weekend together with those who are not doing well in life, you're not likely to get plenty of assistance in the event you attempt to crack loose and also get your thing. Bear in mind; you will become that which you devote the most time and choose that hugely attentively.

1-3. Satisfy your "dead air" period with motivation and affirmation.

If you are in your commute daily, pay attention to your inspirational language or speech. During the time you are doing the driving or dishes, a song to a conversation series that pertains to the kind of small business you are attempting to do. Infuse your life together with the maximum amount of proof and determination as you can. You might have to know that the courses significantly more often than formerly, nevertheless they also may seep to the human brain as time passes, and you are going to wind up behaving on intelligence obtained from people that find at which you would like to become.

Chapter three

The best way to have the results that you desire

Some methods which the mind brings exactly what you want

Almost all of us hope to be great and achieve great things. Yet many people fail to actualize that which they desire. We do not have the financial resources, love, enjoyment, or success within our own lives. However, that which we will need to comprehend is the fact that greatness is within all of us. It's merely up for us to pull on out it of ourselves. Almost everyone is brilliant. All of us simply have to understand how to make us of our intelligence. Decide exactly what you would like.

6 ideas to method the mind to bring everything you want

As a way to acquire that which you would like, you have to decide precisely what you would like from the start. Many people genuinely filthy up in the vital initial measure since they only cannot find the way that it is potential to comprehend the things that they desire -- they do let them want it.

1. **Do not endanger yourself this manner!**

What Boffins discovered about how a brain operates is which you need to decide 1st precisely what you need, until the human brain can find out how to receive it. The moment you fulfill your desires, the mind, and also the world might measure into it.

Are you prepared to get started?

2. Be happy to fight huge desires

After you develop a particular aspiration and go after it, your subconscious mind may think of big concepts to create it take place. You are going to begin employing regulations attraction to pull the individual's resources and changes that you want in your life to turn your fantasy into reality. Enormous fantasies perhaps not merely motivate one, they even induce the others to wish to engage in vast, far too.

3. Establish aims which may stretch you personally

Still another significance in giving yourself consent to proceed following the huge fantasies is the fact that enormous illusions ask that you cultivate to accomplish them. The truth is that at the very long haul, that's the best advantage you have from chasing your fantasies -- perhaps not as far that the outside trappings of satisfying with the romance (a pricey motor vehicle, striking household, heaps of cash and unsuspecting possibilities), however, that you eventually become from the procedure.

As I have observed from the above analysis, the outer symbols of succeeding can be readily discarded. Houses burn down; employers go bankrupt, relationships lead to bankruptcy, cars and trucks get old, and celebrity Jelqing, however, that you have been, whatever you've heard and also the brand-new capabilities you might have grown never move off. These would be the authentic prizes of succeeding. Motivational thinker, Jim Rohn counsels that "you have to decide on an objective huge enough in the procedure for accomplishing, you eventually become someone values."

4. Assistance others

Another thing you are going to find out is when your fantasies include things like assistance to others -- attaining some job which leads to the others -- additionally, it hastens the achievement of your objective. People today would like to participate in something that that will make some difference in the world.

5. Switch your dreams into aims and goals

As soon as you're apparent in that which you would like, you ought to flip just about everything to a quantifiable aim. By measurable, "I am measurable in distance and moment -- only how much and from when. For example, in case you should share with me you wished additional cash, then I'd make a buck and also provide it for you, nevertheless, you'd probably demonstrate, expressing supposed a lot more income --

such as $20,000!" effectively, how am I meant to learn if you don't explain to me personally? Similarly, your supervisor, your buddies, your better half, the human brain -- god, the universe -- cannot determine everything you would like if you don't let them know specifically what exactly it is. What should you want -- and when would you like to buy?

6. Produce your aims down

Write your ends down into more detail and see a listing of aims daily. This will keep your subconscious mind dedicated to what you like. For the much more robust strategy, shut your eyes and give attention to just about every goal and also have, "what's one thing that I really could do now to proceed ahead of the success of the objective?" write your replies and choose the activities.

Manifestation information: the way you can achieve whatever you need in 24-hrs.

Can you still foresee how you want your life to be in the future? Possibly you abide by the legislation of attraction and only cannot conquer dependence? It could be catchy in the beginning, but as soon as you have the hang of this, you could eventually become second nature for you personally. You might not be sure of what the symptom genuinely signifies or perhaps you require clarity about just what the objective of reflection will be! To be able to be successful in your resumes, you want to imagine inside these genuinely.

Thus, it is instructive to note that the intricacies of exactly what the symptom is and the way to attest precisely what you would like. Earlier I talked about my symptom guide on you; let us look at what symptom means and also the way that it performs out.

what exactly does 'manifestation' necessarily mean?

There are several distinct definitions of this phrase attest, however, the most wildly accepted on is stated as "something that's placed to your actual reality by the idea, feelings, emotions, and beliefs".

This usually means that everything you concentrate on is what you're bringing to your reality. You will need emphasis and attest by way of meditation, visualization, or by only using your subconscious or conscious mind.

The following procedure is known as pairing!

For instance, if you've been believing that getting a new job and also dedicated to what you required and also when it, you're thinking and emotions are strong encircling this particular. You may then take to and meditate or imagine your aim, and these assists manifest it in your actuality.

Should you achieve that aim of getting your aspired occupation, you could now say that you have manifested your aspiration into reality. Thus, given you are aware of what symptom signifies, it is the right time and energy to learn how addiction workout.

Just how can manifestation do the job?

As together with all the regulation of attraction, a manifestation is wherever your ideas, along with your energy, may result to your own reality. If you're always feeling down and negative minded, then you definitely will bring and establish power.

The very first action to take if demonstrating is always to have a review of your thinking and emotions. Are you currently feeling unwanted? Can your thinking encircle negativity? If this is the case, you might commence attesting matters which you never desire on your reality. This can be the reason why it is important to keep your mind clean and also have an optimistic spirit once you want to achieve your fantasy.

Manifestation does not merely function with your mind; there must always be a questionnaire of activity in character. This is employing for those tasks that go well with everything it is that you want and visiting the interviews.

Making an attempt to envision your ideas along with feelings of your occupation, this is going to subsequently give you the chance to experience positive and motivated to create such improvements a real possibility. This may then induce one to shoot a few actions and, fundamentally, manifest your aims to your own life.

The way you can manifest whatever in 5 measures

After you browse regulations of attraction, it may sometimes feel as if it's going to take years or months to manifest whatever you want. But specialists urge that if you carefully work your way through 4 different manifestation measures, then it will be potential to have results very early. The truth is that if you're thinking about just how exactly to manifest such a thing within only 24 hours, then you might just want five measures.

Consequently, if you obey this simple reflection guide, you will achieve what you would like in 2-4 hours and less!

(and should you think you might have a reflection block, then you also can take this particular quiz to learn what is energetically keeping back you)

Manifestation measure 1: select everything you would like to manifest

When you decide to achieve something unique, you must try to realize the effect that decision will have on your life. When making attempt to attest something within 2-4 hours, then you need to choose what you think you're able to attest every day.

For instance, there's minimal purpose in which you would like to begin a new firm in 2-4 hours if you don't honestly believe you'll be able to accomplish this aim in time to come. But, you could think you may successfully attest the next step on your travel to some brand-new business every time, at that instance you've placed that since your aim (e.g., to successfully finish a small business program, for yourself a loan which you require, or even find someone to collaborate).

When choosing something to attest, think about these subsequent questions:

Can I genuinely need that, from my own heart of hearts?

How can I reap the benefits of this in particular?

While I consider getting this particular, can it texture proper?

How can it be excellent for me personally and also for others?

Whatever desire ought to function as higher excellent, and also whatever that you would like on your own; many likely something which is a substantial measure on the travel involving an increased reflection aim

Manifestation measure 2: eliminate matters which stand on your way

Regrettably, there is always something preventing you from attaining success. This will not frighten you personally, which is only part of the full manifestation course of action.

Maintain a lookout to all these three common symptom cubes:

Damaging beliefs/mindset

If you're feeling depressed, first thing you have to do is try to develop a positive mindset before you successfully attest anything else. You cannot be emphasizing negativity and hope to achieve great things in your life. Take time and energy to practice. Try out meditation along with differing stress-relief methods.

2. Hazardous folks

Whenever you're focusing on bettering your fantasy, you have to make sure that nobody is drawing you back. Individuals who do not rely on you consistently criticize you or whine of what are cubes that are going to prevent you from accomplishing your very best.

3. Period

Sometimes you only ought to have patience. All you wish for will eventually come to you. Nonetheless, it is going to take place at the proper time as well as to find the ideal explanations. If things are not working out for you at the moment, it will not signify it will. Maintain thinking and maintain working together on your target.

Manifestation measure 4: do something to manifest exactly what you would like

You may devote the rest of your day pretty much alive because you typically want; there are no specific actions you ought to take as a way to earn reflection potential (your goals are what's going to influence your accomplishment). Relatively, as soon as you have finished methods 1 and 2 as clarified previously, you're only awaiting whatever you really would like to look at.

There are some reasons why you might be clubbed fast. Specifically, take into account if you are wondering the procedure; would you not consider you may receive what you ask for because you never believe you ought to have this, or maybe uncertainty if it will be potential to attest employing the law of attraction?

All sorts of negative emotions (e.g., anxiety, anger, anxiety, and uncertainty) or unwanted beliefs may impair your outcomes.

Manifestation measure 5: understand and enjoy

Even though this last measure may not seem that important at first, it could do much to design your reflection potential later on. The essential idea here is you want to completely understand what you need the moment you reach your target. Also, it should not be hard to forget which you just asked what you've have, thus simply take proactive things to do to protect against this.

Return to everything you've had in mind along with what you felt whenever you imagined your preferred thing or results and join those experiences together with all the newest adventure of getting everything you desire. Take into account the tangible evidence you possess that views are all matters, also that believing surely may cause substantial fluctuations on the planet over you.

Even the longer you create the particular connection and highlight it, the higher you end up in manifesting from the foreseeable future (while you are going to substitute unwanted, restricting beliefs and doubts with positive, constructive ideas and emotions).

7 steps to getting what you want from your subconscious mind:

1. Describe your desire.

It is not tricky to get what you want. We've got them every day.

A wide range, all of the moment; point.

Here is a good example. Let's take for example that you are always walking or always take a bus to wherever you go. At a point you got tired of this all. It suddenly happens for you -- that a vehicle could seem excellent. Wonderful!

You have realized that a vehicle is your desire.

Today, you should, do not discount it. Do not shrug off it and say, "yeah, it doesn't just happen". I don't have enough money for it."

2, bear in mind...

You will find unlimited approaches for that your urge to attest! 2. Flake out.

In the event you've been after me by today, you understand that this is an inescapable measure. Now you are interested in being at a relaxed, yet smooth frame of mind.

That's the state of mind that lets that seed of one's goal to become implanted in the subject of one's subconscious mind.

Bear in mind; there's no force that is demanding the following. Force continues to be also counterproductive.

Consider one's unconscious mind as the part of your mind that want the best for you, and also perhaps not a servant to perform your every bidding.

3. Think about it.

Watch yourself with precisely what you want.

You can even get yourself better: find yourself years later needing experiencing that want.

Say, now, you desire a Toyota.

You may get yourself a lot farther into the long-run -- but make the upcoming now on your suspected spectacle.

imagine you are driving your costlier, pricier luxury auto, and laughing because you inform a buddy the way you believed after you've acquired your older Toyota.

Notice how it will work? You may play that yet you desire to. You may merely imagine acquiring possessed the Toyota to get per calendar year for those who don't wish to move too away.

Recall, do not visualize this occurring later on. Ensure it is now, also making it the following.

4. Feel.

Have that the emotions which come in turning into a car operator. Watch yourself while driving and keep your mind on the wheel

Odor the brand-new vehicle stress. Rev these motors.

Imagine visiting with your buddy with all you adoring your brand-new vehicle. Feel the way it seems like see them be happy for you.

5. Do not forget.

Remember when you do not own an automobile? Do you remember when you used to walk to wherever you are going to or take a bus?

Don't forget that moment an auto driving by are you currently dirty drinking water from the torrential rain?

Following is an awesome suggestion in recalling your existing, undesirable conditions as when they took place in the past. Your unconscious mind does not recognize the gap!

It does not recognize what you believe about previously; it is clear what is occurring today!

Therefore, it functions to create what is occurring today, before.

A lot of people often utilize this method backward.

Plus, it functions well! Typically, it's "recall when this bunch of processors had been just a dollar"

Watch that simply hammers it house for these. That matters are becoming even worse. However, you may remember times when things are in bad condition, indicating now, they indeed are far superior!

6. Value.

show genuine appreciation for people who helped you realize this dream

Be grateful to those who create the auto, the cash that arrived or whoever gave you the auto, or anything.

Have that the admiration, for no more being a real pedestrian.

7. Let it go.

As natural finish that is using permitting go.

You go as you understand that you have your automobile. You know you have your car or truck as you lent yourself in creativeness.

Chapter four

The portentous power of one's unconscious

Can be your mind to bring everything you need

What exactly is my unconscious?

Back in Freud's psychoanalytic concept of character, the subconscious mind can be a reservoir of emotions, ideas, recommendations, and recollections, which out our conscious recognition. Most of the content of our unconscious mind are either improper or disagreeable, like emotions of melancholy, anxiety, or battle.

Can there be an unconscious?

The answer is no... These items while the subconscious mind; we're just two adventures which we're mindful, yet many others which individuals aren't knowledgeable, which is we're not unconscious.

The unconscious mind: under the top of recognition

When believing about their subconscious mind, it could be useful to evaluate your accountant to an iceberg—that which over the drinking water reflects alert awareness while beneath the drinking water demonstrates the subconsciousness.

Consider the way the iceberg would seem if you could view it in its entirety. Merely a small region of the iceberg is over the drinking water. Everything you are unable to see from your point of view is that the immense quantity of ice which is made up of most of the plateau, submerged deep underneath from water.

The matters that reflect our mindful recognition are only "the end of this iceberg." the remaining part of the info that's out conscious awareness depends on the top. While this info may perhaps not be reachable knowing, it exerts a present impact on behavior.

Freud thought that a lot of our feelings, needs, and emotions had been held outside of recognition. why? Because they implied, they were only overly threatening. Freud considered that these hidden wants and fantasies create themselves understood throughout fantasies and slips of the tongue (aka "Freudian slips").

What're unconscious facts brought into recognition?

Also, there are some various ways which advice in the subconscious mind may be attracted into conscious recognition, by Freud.

Free association: Freud also thought he would attract these subconscious feelings to awareness throughout using an approach referred to as a free institution. He requested sufferers to unwind and state anything came into mind with no thought of just how trivial, irrelevant, or uncomfortable it may be. By minding such flows of the idea, Freud considered he can discover the contents of their subconscious mind where repressed wants and debilitating childhood reminiscences take place.

Fantasy interpretation: Freud also implied that visions were just another path to the subconscious mind. While the advice in the subconscious mind could sometimes be found in fantasies, he felt it had been regularly in a disguised form. Fantasy translation frequently entails assessing the written material of the fiction (called the manifest content material) to take to discover the concealed, subconscious significance of the tale (that the latent content material). Freud also thought that visions proved to be a kind of desire satisfaction. Due to this, subconscious recommendations could be voiced at waking existence, he considered they locate saying in fantasies.

Criticisms

The most thought of the occurrence of this whoever has never been devoid of controversy. A lot of researchers have repeatedly resisted that the idea and questions that there's genuinely a subconscious mind in the slightest.

Recently, within the area of cognitive psych, scientists have centered on computerized and suggested purposes of characterizing matters which were earlier credited to the subconscious mind. As stated by the particular approach, you can find some cognitive features that happen out of our conscious comprehension. This exploration may perhaps not encourage Freud's conceptualization of their subconscious mind. Nevertheless, it will not offer signs that matters that individuals aren't mindful of knowingly could affect our behaviors.

Unlike ancient psychoanalytic methods to the subconscious, study over the area of cognitive psych is firmly pushed by scientific investigations and practical information behind the occurrence of those automated cognitive procedures.

A word out of the obvious fact

Even though Sigmund Freud didn't devise this notion of subconscious mind and he did popularize it into the purpose, it is chiefly related to all his psychoanalytic theories. The concept of the subconscious mind has been playing a part in psychology since researchers attempt to comprehend the method by which the mind works out conscious comprehension.

Unconscious mind

The subconscious mind contains those procedures from the brain that occur mechanically and aren't readily available to introspection and comprise idea procedures, recollections and passions, and motives.

While these processes exist nicely underneath the face mindful consciousness, they're supposed to apply a positive affect behavior. The expression has been appreciated since the 18th century German affectionate thinker fried rich Schelling and afterward introduced to English from the poet and essayist Samuel Taylor Coleridge

Empirical evidence indicates that sneaky phenomena comprise repressed beliefs, computerized abilities, subliminal perceptions, along with automatic response and even complexes, concealed phobias, and wants.

The idea had been popularized by the Austrian neurologist and also psycho-analyst Sigmund Freud. Back in the psychoanalytic principle, unconscious procedures are known to be most straight represented in fantasies, in addition at slides of their tongue along with jokes.

So the subconscious mind could be viewed the way to obtain fantasies and computerized notions (the ones who arise with no apparent origin) the repository of abandoned memories (that can continue to be obtainable to understanding in a subsequent period) and also the locus of implied expertise (what that we have learned well we perform these without any thinking).

It's been contended that different part of the mind have influenced consciousness. Included in these are unconsciousness for being a personalized custom, staying oblivious along with instinct. Phenomena linked to semi-consciousness include things like an awakening, suggested memory, subliminal messages, trances, hypnagogic along with hypnosis. Even though sleeping, sleep-walking, dreaming, delirium, and comas can prove the existence of subconscious processes, those procedures have been noticed as signs or symptoms in contrast to the subconscious mind.

The presence of the subconscious – Some critics

The best way to make use of your unconscious mind to accomplish your aims

The most effective method to modify your behavior to become better is by always getting the job done in conjunction together with your subconscious mind.

It was concluded in January how a lot of people left their new year's resolutions this past calendar, however, have broken these?

Possibly we told me we would work out a lot more, or even spend time together with all our kids, or never becoming mad all of the moment. But we are no closer to those aims than we ever were earlier.

Additionally, it turns out this part of the problem could be how we create all these settlements: they rely upon our mindful decision-making procedures. We only place a fantastic aim to do things otherwise, and also, we leave it in the. But knowledge must inform us that unique goals tend to be inadequate.

Within my book, until you recognize it's present most of the manners our private boat of first goals could get ignored route from the powerful subconscious motives and environmental cues which likewise influence that which we are doing. Due to the fact that we aren't mindful of those unconscious impacts, we do not know anything to counteract them. Nevertheless, they indeed are similar to the winds and currents, which affects a boat's path only as far while the captain's rudder. Dismiss them, and you might float more now from the senior wreck into the stones.

The very first question to ask when a resolution is neglected is: how can I genuinely need to modify? If you are being honest with yourself, you, in fact, desire to maintain ingesting, or overeating, or even maybe performing exercises. And the ones would like are about to reevaluate the fantastic goals of one's resolutions.

By recognizing those subconscious effects on people, we raise the sum of completely free will that we have. When we refuse that those impacts exist, we then have been in their twenties and have less control than we all think we do. However, what is better is the fact that as we realize the method by which they do the job, we can turn those mental powers into our advantage.

A long time of lab study and pragmatic presentations in real life preferences have shown the power of mindful "implementation goals." How do they work?

Ourselves in certain traditions, we can eliminate clues and chances from types and then replace our subconscious impulses having welcome messages that are alert.

This way, we may often make use of the power of the subconscious mind...and also have a lot of superior chances of preserving these new year's resolutions.

Unconscious mind

Though we are mindful of what's going on in our mind, we have got zero concepts about what exactly advice is saved from the subconscious mind.

The subconscious mind is made up of all types of heavy and upsetting stuff that we will certainly need to be maintained from consciousness as they are exceedingly threatening to admit totally.

The subconscious mind functions like a repository, a 'cauldron' of crude fantasies and urge kept in the bay and also blindsided from the preconscious place. For example,

Freud (1915) unearthed that a few occurrences and wants were frequently overly scary or debilitating because of his sufferers to admit, also felt that such advice had been locked off from the subconscious mind. This sometimes happens using the procedure of repression.

Crucial assessment

To begin with, psych has been biased about the notion of mental procedures functioning at a subconscious stage. More psychologists developed to become more technological in their technique (e.g., behaviorists) that the idea of the subconscious mind has shown that a source of substantial frustration for the reason that it defies target explanation, also so is tough to test or quantify.

Nevertheless, the difference between psychology and psycho-analysis has become clearer over time, and also the concept of the subconscious mind has turned into an essential focal point in psych. For instance, cognitive psych has recognized subconscious procedures, for example as behavioral memory (Tulving, 1972), automated processing (Bargh & Chartrand, 1999; Stroop, 1935), along with societal psychology has demonstrated the significance of proposed processing (Greenwald & Banaji, 1995). These kinds of empirical research also have shown the function of unconscious processes in human behavior.

Chapter five

Mental recovery methods

Option fixing methods to think about

Even the way people cure disease, alleviate soothe, and sickness pain is slowly changing with lots of people opting to add alternative curing processes with traditional medication. If a person feels like he/she is not feeling fine, the person should really visit an experienced healthcare practitioner. Still, they might also consider making use of different medication which could help. Here would be 16 substitute curing methods, which may be of great benefit.

1. Therapeutic massage and reflexology

Massage and reflexology are currently believed to be a more mainstream technique of curing, have been considered other treatment options. These two could get tremendous health gains, notably massage if used to govern debilitating muscular tissues. Reflexology operates based on that you will find stress points at the foot that are related solely to various part of your human body. Also, dealing together with such strain points might help ease problems from the affiliated physiological locations.

2. Homeopathy

Homeopathic remedies operate together with the basic principle which your system is capable of curing alone. Medicines which comprise of little quantity of chemicals that led to the very first disease have been accepted, coping with all the impression that anything generated a condition may additionally help cure it.

3. Reiki recovery

Even the westerners exercise of reiki operates by balancing the amount of energy within your system. Even a reiki profession puts their fingers only above your human anatomy, never earning contact, to secure healing with their body for a station to get key worldwide energy stream into the individual.

4. Acupuncture

Acupuncture are tiny needles being inserted into your skin in numerous defined points across the whole body. Acupuncture started in china and is now a favorite type of another curing across the globe.

5. Aroma-therapy

Aroma-therapy is where specific scents are inhaled to attract your mind body and soul into balance. This efficient smells are extracted from plants and herbs where the finished product is in oil form

6. Hypnosis

Hypnosis works when an individual gets into a schizophrenic state of mind. A hypnotic state can be a modified type of understanding that leaves the affected individual more vulnerable to the powers of the proposal. It's frequently utilized to alter harmful customs, treat migraines, and cut back ache.

7. Detox

Detox works by cleansing the human anatomy. Harmful toxins are removed mainly from your body. A stiff diet has to have been followed closely to get a fixed quantity of time, as a way to provide your human body time and energy to satisfactorily flush out all of the poison in your system strategically.

8. Meditation

Meditation involves assessing your mind for undesired ideas which helps an individual to become more focused and present. This will aid in the procedure of particular conditions caused by stress and melancholy. It may likewise be utilized to relieve soreness.

9. Laughter remedy

Magnets are broadly utilized in other medications. This method is dependent on the thought that electromagnetic areas might help circulate and stabilize energy quantities of the human body.

10. Counseling

Counselling and other types of psychotherapy do the job of altering the thinking of a person which might help heal mental disorders. Such method is often utilized when someone is stressed, depressed or have emotional problems, and dependence.

11. Sound curing

Sound healing works by hearing sounds or music, which can be soothing and also improve your overall body's defects into your optimum condition essential for curing.

12. Hydro-therapy

Hydro-therapy uses water to both heal and also stop ailments and illnesses. It has lots of diverse applications of drinking water, which include saunas, steam baths, and salt punches, immersion bathrooms, and irrigation.

13. Yoga

Yoga can help balance your entire body and mind, also increase muscular features, strength, and stability.

14. Crystal therapeutic

Crystals could be put on the problem areas and chakra things to rebalance your overall body's energies.

15. Psychic curing

Psychic or religious recovery works by using rituals. Prayers or incantations are found in such a category, together with individual curative institutes.

16. Color therapeutic

Colors are related to various parts of your anatomy. It's believed that visualizing the appropriate color, combined recurrent side vulnerability into this shade, donning outfits of this shade, and ingestion food items of this shade might accelerate curing procedures.

Spiritual retrieval methods i make an effort to assist heal my melancholy

Being fully gloomy is hard. Becoming identified as gloomy is much worse.

When I was diagnosed with melancholy in Nov 2011, I was an 18-year-old child starting up her life as a freshman at higher institution. I used to be within my fantasy university off at your home, having a partial scholarship and fantasies, too, as someone else. I'd like nothing at all to become miserable about, however, that I dropped right into it.

Later afflicted by emotions of depression, anxiety, nervous breakdown, depression, and even seclusion, I had to sought for help. It had been just roughly 14 days within these emotions I seen my own faculty's mental wellness office. However, I'd no concept about exactly what I had been becoming. Once I got my identification, I realized that the simple fact which I had to begin attending equally group and individual therapy periods.

Having gone for treatment for about two decades ago, I understood that getting the constraint of my mental wellbeing wasn't the endpoint. I heard that melancholy proved to be a lifelong struggle, and also just like a habit, relapsing was consistently a possibility. As a result of it, I embraced four religious therapeutic methods to aid me at the times of my everyday program.

Amethyst recovery gemstones

This is somehow a new procedure I've experimented. Having been through a big operation exactly where three harmless microbes had been taken in the gut last year in January, the condition of the health of my body needed a significant strain in my mental wellness. Two amethyst stones had been awarded to me personally by my grandma. I started rubbing those two stones on each aspect of my mind (respectfully) every time that I sensed my anxiety creeping in at the house to get a couple of moments. Gradually they helped to facilitate the mental pressure that I had been going through. Also, I possess an amethyst necklace that I use.

Incense sticks

Sometimes the most relaxing place to be would be our household. May it's truly be a long evening of job, or only the overall relaxation of having within your residence, becoming indoors the four partitions that you simply telephone your home would be your optimal/optimally location to grow. Once you treat mental health problems they will just help you heal. That's the reason why aroma-therapy proved to be a fantastic healing technique because of me personally. Each time I feel as if my emotions are still becoming a lot and I'm in the home, my alternative action involves burning incense sticks and light candles to reduce my worries.

Meditation novels

As a preventive step, I like reading meditation books and posts, which help direct my mind towards my meditation clinics. While I've electronic networking to assist lead my meditation, I understand that examining helps introduce all out of the more powerful view. Also, this is a means to find mindfulness believing on days when you've got the program, which lets you see pieces and bits.

Mindful consuming

Eating three times a day can equally be significant and advocated; however, the number of times we can try to eat these meals interrupted from the time limitations of this evening event or occasions upward beforehand? After understanding this, I went on a strict diet. I eat about 5 to 6 times per time and percentage out my foods to healthy and equal numbers each moment; point. This provides me with something to anticipate and become thankful to.

Ways to use your mind to strengthen and heal your body

1. If you plan to secure improved, it just might occur on time

There is a between how your brain functions along with how your entire body feels. And only because you can utilize your own body to lower your emotional distress, you may employ the mind to advance your physique.

By altering the manner, you assume and accept control of everything conveys your mind can boost your health of your body and also your general wellbeing. Favorable pondering won't fix all. However, a nutritious mindset can be just a central aspect of healthful human anatomy. Listed below are 7 ways by which you can employ your mind to market bodily wellbeing:

Create your remedies longer successfully by anticipating them to do the job.

Studies have shown that the placebo influence affects the efficacy of the treatment. If a person lets you know a pill can fix the aggravation, you are more inclined to come across the treatment method beneficial --even though the tablet computer has been a sugar tablet. Whether you are looking for a bodily remedy to get a terrible knee or you are visiting a chiropractor to heal the pain on your spine, the way you see those treatment options will continue to work may be useful compared to the procedure by themselves. Before you experience all types of treatment methods, believe in every one of the causes that the process is probably going to provide help.

2. Sleeping improved by composing in a gratitude journal.

If you are suffering from sleeplessness, a gratitude journal may be the optimal healing method. A few scientific tests have connected gratitude to improved quality and much more sustained snooze. Before going to bed, try to acknowledge three things you are thankful to get and then compose them at a gratitude diary. conjuring up emotions of thankfulness before you go to sleep can make possible the chances of having a fantastic night's nap.

3. Live more by concentrating on your purpose in everyday life.

Feeling as you, own an awareness of function could raise the duration of one's own life. Scientific research shows that people who see themselves to have a purpose in life are more inclined to stay healthy and live a longer life. If work provides you with a motive or you also detect significance by devoting your time and effort, be sure everything you are doing things. Feeling as you own grounds to escape from bed daily may be the trick to endurance.

4. Be optimistic and encourage your immunity.

Studies have shown that favorable men and women tend to fall sick. For years, quite a few investigators believed that the boost in resistance originated in the simple fact optimistic everyone was likely to manage this wellness. However, recent scientific studies have proven an optimistic prognosis is what affects immunity. Seeking the bright aspect leaves you not as inclined to receive yourself a disease or cold as strangers retain your immunity system acting in its summit.

5. Intense getting older with meditation.

Meditation gives a generous buffer contrary to the damaging ramifications stress could get within your system. Few scientific tests show that meditation reduces down the rate in which a person age. Meditation can assist you in appearing young. Also, it might help you in reducing the chances of celiac illness.

Researchers guess teaching kiddies to meditate can offer lifelong added benefits. But regardless of what era you're, it is certainly not too late to get a few wellness advantages from meditation.

6. Assemble muscle mass by picturing your self-exercising out.

Imagine should you might get lover by imagining yourself lifting weights? Nicely, scientists have discovered that mental vision can assist you in getting muscle with raising a finger. 1 analyze unearthed people who guessed themselves working-out was also equipped to attain 2 to 4 percent higher muscular energy. Individuals who lifted weights noticed improved consequences; however, even the investigation shows that mental teaching might offer real variations to mass muscle tissue.

7. Decrease your chance of coronary illness from discussing.

In a situation where you want to have a much healthy heart, then consider some funny comical. Studies show bliss reduces stress hormones, improves "excellent" cholesterol, also reduces stomach irritation. Most likely, laughter is actually that the optimal/optimally medication --the most results of bliss past 2 to 4 hours per day.

Chapter six

The subconscious motions at the course of existence

Helpful tips to living your daily life consciously

A lifetime of selection would be a lifetime of mindful activity. A life lived of likelihood is now that a lifetime of sub-par invention.

Just as you can, I attempt to live life by bringing in my understanding to what's bubbling upward out of my unconsciousness.

I attempt to clean that the fog during that we now often ramble, to observe where I am going to produce mindful decisions alternatively of automatic ones.

Can you have a sense where you are drifting during lifestyle, and maybe not moving at the rate you would like to go? Or you never discover the way you got where you live now?

Living a conscious life puts you in control of your own life, around believing concerning your own decisions as opposed to earning them thought, around using a lifetime we need in the place of opting to get the one which disturbs us.

In case you are drifting through existence, or sense out of command, or do not understand the way you have right here... Determining to call home consciously would possibly be the one most essential thing that you need to do.

Are you currently alive unconsciously?

Ask the following questions...Should you realize that you are saying yes to a lot of these, you may want to look at trying aware residing:

Are you currently at work which you dropped right into in contrast to the task that you like?

2. Are you currently really doing things which are awarded for your requirements than that which you would like to do?

3. Are you currently really spending your time busy with work instead of that which is related to your times?

4. Do you want that you can devote additional hours with family members?

5. will you add weight as you were eating the exact food which you've been searching for ages and trapped in an area of exercising?

6. Can you wind up living from deal to pay or at cash, never realizing exactly how you spent your money?

7. Can you wind up wasting your time accomplishing things which can be crucial in the place of emphasizing completing precisely the issues which are essential?

8. Can you proceed throughout your times, maybe not thinking about everything you would like from living and also ways correctly to receive it?

In the event, you replied "no more" to each one of these inquiries; you are most likely already alive knowingly. Also, you don't require this informative article in the slightest. For all those that like to call home time after time, keep reading.

The best way to be living consciously

It is maybe not at all something that you may change immediately. Living a conscious life is a lifestyle, skill, and artwork. It is

Here are some fundamental hints which have worked for me:

1. Ensure representing in your own life a routine. If you maintain a diary or create serving on your daily life section of one's day regular, or just have a weekly session in which you examine your life or take a moment off from your place of work to think about your life... It truly is crucial that you simply devote matters a few notions. Ability.

2. At a minimum, once every calendar year, review or set your daily life aims or things

you hope to achieve. What would you like to achieve in your life? What's significant for your requirements personally? Precisely what does one would like your own life to be like? And will you arrive? Write it down, and also maintain it someplace you may observe it usually, and also do it.

3. Additionally, examine your relationships. Most folks we adore are one of the essential items within our own resides, though maybe the just significant matters. You should consider your relationships. Do you spend plenty of time together with the people you care about? Would you reveal your admiration, in their opinion? Can there be a way to better your relationship? Can you forgive or emphasize whatever else? Are there any hurdles that may be taken off? Communication that should be made better?

Additionally, examine your relationships together with the others, like co-workers.

4. Be careful of the impact you have around the people around you. Just how can precisely what you do, how that which you eat, and the way your home is, impact that the surroundings? How can it influence inferior people in third world countries? How can this influence the bad, the powerless, the voiceless? How can this impact your environment? Your own life gets a consequence if you contemplate any of it or never. Be conscious.

5. Contemplate the actual cost implication of everything you buy. We frequently purchase things without actually considering what we're doing precisely what they genuinely expense. Sure, why it is only $30... No real problem, correct? However, that thirty

dollars could reflect a few hours of one's own life. You'll never return. You might not need to devote your life-generating revenue on purchases that are fiddling? Is that precisely what you desire related to your own life? Worth a few ideas, I presume. Go through your money or your living for longer.

6. Contemplate the actual expenses of these things in your life. Our own lives are full of products... Our residences our places of work... And past only the price of getting the items, this substance has a toll on people. The things in our own life have to be carefully arranged, cleaned, transferred, shot together move... It takes up the space in our personal experience, it's visible stress. After we are going to need to eliminate it, either type through it all, take care, and energy to throw it away or recycle it or contribute it. If

using the material isn't worth most, that, subsequently do away with this.

7. Review how you spend your leisure time. Right up until we perform a moment study, also maintain a record of your daily life, also though it's only for a couple of days do not know just how exactly we devote our own time. And should people conduct a research our period, it might be quite astonishing. Of course, should we discover just how exactly we're spending our time today, we will make conscious decisions to improve how we devote our period later on. For part-time period monitoring, strive saving time.

8. Research yourself. In a dirty manner. Just take a while to consider the type of man or woman that you are; what exactly your worth would be. If your home is life by all those values. The way to treat people. The

best way to cure yourself. Look at that: exactly what exactly do you really would like people to share with you whenever you perish? Read the secret to dying joyful.

Chapter seven

The best way to make use of the power of the subconscious mind

The best way to make use of the power of the unconscious mind to resist

Your subconscious mind is a powerful drive to be reckoned with. It constitutes approximately 95 percent of your brainpower and also manages all the entire body making sure of its functionality, away from breathing and eating into making and digesting reminiscences.

Visualize your good results

The very first and very significant variable you will have to think about when it concerning tapping into your subconscious mind, which means you may triumph in whatever you will always be to imagine what you would like or exactly what your objective will be. As stated by analysis conducted in 1996 in Michigan state college, 46 percent of patients that received evaluations in graphics were somewhat likely to follow along with their homecare program.

Apply getting in touch using the mind

Meditation has been famous for many years and has been recognized to fully be a fantastic means to acquire in touch using your subconscious mind to learn the way that it is working out. Practicing ten minutes every day could have a positive aspects in the way that your brain operates along with the wellness of one's health.

Jennifer Olson, a lifestyle author, stocks, "work out can be so significant, maybe not just for the body although the condition of mind. I typically begin my afternoon having a 20-minute yoga session, also followed closely by a 10-minute meditation session after I escape from bed, simply to have off the day for the optimal/optimally beginning".

Commence growing your writing capabilities

Using a very new idea, composing out of the subconscious mind can appear to be an abstract idea. If you anticipate starting a daily journal and sometimes maybe producing a narrative, you would certainly be astounded your subconscious mind performs a vital role in that which we compose and hence is an important means to keep in touch together.

Our subconscious mind surpasses thus much advice and thoughts, a lot will not pass through our mind, which makes it an excellent resource the moment it regards getting down ideas in writing or onto a monitor. Additionally, composing permits one to accomplish your subconscious emotions and notions. Internet sites like condition of composing and also academic advisor involve some fantastic tools it's possible to utilize when it has to do with forming a composing custom. This is a powerful method.

Establish aims

You may aim currently existing on your mind, which you believe once in a while; however, that will not signify they are goals you're planning to get. As stated in a research conducted by Dr. Gail Matthews, 43 percent of individuals that regularly jot their targets and fantasies are much more inclined to reach them.

Michelle Parker, a lifetime trainer and founder of cite it in exclaims, "by writing your targets and putting them even when you jot the exact item every day, the action of reading and writing them back yourself is always a significant means to receive your subconscious mind based on exactly what your conscious mind wishes for, also it might begin getting steps in to allow it to come about."

Care for your self

That is a broad topic. However, it is important that you simply check out if you would like to ensure success. Looking yourself signifies consuming a nutritious diet, exercising regularly, drinking adequate water daily, and also making the optimal/optimally decision to check following the entire body as well as mind.

Through the way you appear in your physique, most suitably, you can make sure you will be functioning into an optimum amount, which makes it a no-brainer that the subconscious and conscious minds are doing work in their best to produce your fantasies a real possibility.

Feelings on "the best way to make use of the power of the unconscious mind to resist.

Sub aware is something that we does not manage straight. It's their state of mind that regulates all of our activities. Means to restrain this together with all our conscious mind is hopeless due to the fact our conscious mind is a subset of the subconscious mind.

Some methods to examine and restrain sub conscious mind:

1. Maintain your breath, believing ardently of exactly what you would like your subconscious mind to become. Maintaining your breath generates a crisis. That's whenever the subconscious mind will come to actions as you ardently think it gets signs; also, it might be molded.

2. After your conscience.

3. That is an expression" for those who do things continuously to get 40 weeks; you must keep on to get this done without even attempt". When you do something, your subconscious mind records the activity also proceeds play with it during that time given.

Fundamentally, I'd state that unconscious is also a part of you personally. It's only that you just don't need the use of it. However, once you want to alter it together with your campaign, it frees for your requirements personally as it goes to you personally.

The way to utilize your unconscious mind power

Most of the people are attentive to the occurrence of the subconscious mind. In essence, we don't necessarily understand exactly what it is, what exactly it does, or the way correctly, we can learn how to perfect it.

The fact remains that the power of the subconscious mind is a remarkable ally for those who grasp it. But in case it stays untamed, it may induce the management of one's own life in undesirable manners.

What is your sub conscious mind?

The subconscious mind is perhaps not fanciful. It's somewhat right, significant portion of you personally. Also, it makes it possible for you to unlock powers that you never thought you had.

It's very liked a super computer set in place to assist you make your life adventures.

During your lifetime, you mind is programmed with idea customs and beliefs. Exactly enjoy some of your new habits, the notions which you've replicated to yourself have grown traditions.

There is no actual gap between the habit of linking your sneakers and also the tendency of pondering on yourself at a sure method.

What does the unconscious mind you?

The unconscious mind has a fantastic effect in our own lives. However, we frequently tend to forget it is even there.

The subconscious mind can act as a memory card. A lot of those memories have been saved underneath the top of both your conscious mind and so are concealing at the subconscious mind that outlets them is about to renew them if required.

We now can put away virtually everything in our subconscious mind, if a memory, or an earlier adventure, or even maybe repressed injury.

The best way can the unconscious mind do the job?

Repetition creates dependency. All these mental customs have been united along with your adventures to produce a remarkably intricate system of faith that helps you in reconnecting with the whole world.

The subconscious mind does not do some other creative believing. That isn't its job.

it can't differentiate between what's "fanciful" and what's "true" any idea you replicate or visible graphic you make and bear on the mind are cases of this "running system" your software in your subconscious mind.

The best way to exercise your subconscious power?

The real fact, in addition to your thoughts and emotions, is only flaws of energy.

Energy "packets" known as quanta, may act in any manner which they're influenced with additional quanta. This is referred to the means the energy of one's mind sways things.

Everything you give attention to is exactly what you bring.

Thus, take into account your interior address. what is it real that the mind panic?

Should you inform yourself, day outside?

And what exactly does your mind perform if you introduce a new idea that's in battle using your subconscious programming?

The majority of the moment, we aren't conscious of our interior address.

We proceed through our times -- the majority of our activities and address patterns are not anything but regurgitated info saved from the subconscious mind.

Yes, this makes life straight forward. Try to foresee how challenging it is to take into consideration just how you can tie your shoes whenever you'd to accomplish it. It has a whole lot of mental work that has been automatic!

How can I trigger my subconscious mind?

Being aware of one's internal address provides you with the info which you want to perfect mind.

In case you are in a situation you do not like, it is since you've been believing and sense in a manner that's directed the mind in a particular way, and that's wherever your own life is led!

Thus, if you eventually become attentive to the character of your internal language, you may imprint a new programming and also totally alter the management of one's own life.

It may be gruesome, but enjoyable at the same time to appreciate how great your opinions are still in displaying your circumstances! The subconscious mind works on custom.

Thus, by devoting favorable, positive, "can-do" notions repeatedly until finally, they develop customs, you are going to exchange the previous traditions and make nerve pathways predicated on favorable "I will be/do/have" believing.

Alter originates from inside.

You may shift tasks, end relationships, proceed, but should you "change the mind" from inside of, you are going only to draw the same. Or your changes will probably be temporary. It will likely soon be the" same substance, unique deal with or a spot of occupation..."

Meditation would be the way to turn into conducive to an internal universe and the graphics that you like to paint.

A day-to-day meditation clinic may completely change your life since you know the inner earth, grasp the mind, and match your dominant thoughts.

You may be surprised at the number of ideas you come up with time after time drives you towards what you like. However, by everyday exercise, you can finalize the most suitable programming.

You will detect synchronicity anyplace and your life will be exceptionally great as the outside globe becomes a mirror to your brand-new awesomeness you maintain on your subconscious mind!

The power of 'I am evident'

Self-evident means that the deficiency of perception of your talents and abilities. However, it goes considerably farther and quicker compared to that.

Self-evident is in the heart. It is the manifestation of inadequacy.

Self-evident can attest in a variety of ways. However, it often held sub-conscious beliefs published from youth traumatization.

The actual question would be: how exactly can we be rid of this?

Legendary transformational hypnotherapist, Marisa Peer, stocks several powerful words which have the capacity to battle along with prevent self-uncertainty.

All these statements have also changed the lifestyles of tens of thousands of this mind valley tribe.

Chapter eight

The unconscious mind is an accomplice of your success

Get a handle on your brain

Once your brain is set out at a black box (your skull), and you'll be able to ensure it is believing whatever you desire. Instead of one other way around. "clear up for joyful " and also" buddha's brain," make clear the mindset and even the science supporting this.

Trick

It's surprising how we fool ourselves or the way somebody else could mislead you. Go through "the science of purchasing " or "filter bubble." or only consider just how addicted we're our telephones.

Inquire your unconscious for assistance

You may as well be responsible for to have controller; you require assistance of one's subconscious mind. The stories of this miracle-working powers of one's unconscious mind happen to be in existence for quite a very long time. Inquire. Also, it'll give you. That's my slogan.

The power of the unconscious mind

"The power of the unconscious mind" with Joseph murphy presents several tips. The boundless intellect in your subconscious mind may show you all that you want to understand each time plus point-of distance, given that you might be open-minded and more responsive. I'd guess that stream is more closely linked to that and also to provide you with a few stats:

The power

Aware processing may simply manage roughly 12033 pieces of advice at the same time. This is simply not substantial. Playing some other individual can take nearly 60 pieces. But, subconscious processing (= leak) can take manage a lot of task at the same time. The result is a 200 percent improvement in imagination, a 490 percent enhancement in learning, also a five 500 percent increase in earnings. To put it differently, your subconscious mind can be a super-computer in boundless contact lifetime and immense knowledge.

The key

It's universally accepted that anything you impress your subconscious mind is voiced upon the monitor of distance because of condition, adventure, as well as even event.

The long-run remains on the mind

Over ninety percentage of one's mental life is subconscious—the outer mirrors of the interior. The topical activity follows inside actions. Your potential is on the mind today, dependent on your habitual thinking and beliefs. Your unconscious mind can be that your novel of living.

You know that which you believe

You then become what you believe. Your beliefs or idea in your mind generate consequences. You can establish those results. The procedure is quite easy.

Inquire, sleep and feel

As your subconscious mind never again rests or sleeps, which means you may also make it function for you. feed your subconscious mind with something excellent to focus on as you shed to slumber. You want far more snooze. Sleep attracts counselor. Many replies to your problems come back to us now if we have been sound asleep. The mind will likely respond.

Decree wellness, along with your subconscious mind will set it. In doing this, comfort is critical. "easy does it" don't let yourself get worried about means and details; however, imagine the outcome. Acquire the texture of this joyful remedy for your problem if it's wellness, financing, or even occupation. Rush together using the profound certainty it is completed. Imagine and launch.

A sense of wellbeing generates wellness. The sensation of riches produces riches. How do you believe? A guy that is always thinking about money will be surrounded with what he requires.

This publication says there are three measures to victory

1. The very first step to greatness would always be to locate what you would like to accomplish, then do it.

2. The 2nd step to achievement would always be to concentrate on a few specific divisions of job and also learn much more about this than anybody.

3. The next thing has become the most essential one particular. You have to make sure that the thing you wish to do will not redound for a victory. Try not to be greedy; nonetheless, it has to reward humankind. Your notion has to be published with all the aim of boon or functioning the whole world.

Good results

A prosperous individual enjoys his job along with expresses himself thoroughly. For those who learn how to utilize the powers of mind, also whenever you're expressing yourself-care and committing your talents into others, then you're around the path to authentic achievements.

The methods

The first part of communicating your clarified motivation, notion, or graphic on this deeper mind is always to unwind, trap the eye, catch nonetheless, and also be more silent. The next step would be to try to see what you like—adding a picture in your subconscious mind. Possess the self-confidence which the clear answer consistently arrives, as long as you expect that the operating of one's deep soul.

Peaceful your mind

This is another easy strategy that you can make use of to get assistance in almost any topic: silent your mind but the human anatomy. Inform your anatomy to flake out; it's to comply. It's no volition, initiative, or timid brains. Your own body is an emotional disc that lists your beliefs and beliefs.

Concentrate

Ready your mind and focus your mind in finding the solution to your problem. Attempt to fix it along with your awake mind. Assume how pleased you will certainly be with all the ideal resolution.

The key to advice

The key to advice or right action to take is always to mentally dedicate yourself to this perfect answer, and soon, you detect the response to you personally. The reply would be an atmosphere, an internal consciousness, an overpowering relationship where you are aware you just know.

Meditation

Any publication on meditation will still tell you the same thing. Or see "the amazing job of one's life." believe nice and high traces. Whenever you could be calm, joyful, joyful, and accomplishing precisely what you like to do, then you're profitable. Duplicate this term, "victory," yourself usually with beliefs and certainty, and you're going to be under an unconscious compulsion to be successful certainly. Think subtle and subtle traces.

Be expecting the optimal/optimally

Count on the finest, and also always the very best things will come to you. If you're producing a book, play, or novel, or you are working within an innovation, talk with some subconscious mind during nighttime time. Declare boldly that its wisdom, and power have been directing, and even showing for one of personally the perfect drama, book, publication, and provide you with an ideal option whichever it can be. Wonders may take place.

$$H + e\,r = m$$

In a certain manner, this publication is still shut to "the god formulation: a straightforward clinically verified pattern which has changed countless lives founded by Jeffery A. Martin:

Visualizations + emotion + release = materialization

After building your visualizations you only ought to utilize optimistic notions and objective, and you also ought to view your motivation as being yours, so you need to believe that it come into fruition. Also, you should publish, i.e., inquire about your subconscious. It'll materialize.

Fortunate men and women

Jeffrey martins also had something to say about blessed men and women. Lucky men and women crank out their very own fantastic luck by way of four primary fundamentals. They can be proficient in creating and noticing opportunities, make lucky decisions by following their instinct, make self-fulfilling prophecies via positive expectations, and adopt a resilient attitude that transforms bad luck into good.

The conclusion of lack

Or see "the ending of lack. regular withdrawal in awareness signs and also the confusion and noise of routine alive can be a kind of snooze; i.e., you also eventually become ill in the entire world of their sensations and also living towards the intellect and power of one's subconscious mind.

Pick joy

You have to choose the delights. Ensure it is a custom to become joyful. You should make a decision to be happy. Why choose to be unhappy? The realm of enjoyment would be on your feeling and thought. Get contentment to function as a crop of a calm mind. Nothing may disturb you but also your thoughts.

Several other pearls of knowledge out of" the power of the unconscious mind."

Stress

Do what you're scared to do, and also the passing of fear is specified. Stress has a negative effect on the mind. Supplant it using a good notion. The most fantastic regulation of substitution could be your response to panic. All you panic gets its solution at the shape of one's appetite. If you're ill, then you still would like wellbeing. If you're within the jail of anxiety, then you want liberty. Try to always have a positive mindset towards everything, focus your mind on positive and nice things only and also be aware your subconscious mind replies to you consistently. It fails.

Acquiring older

Mind and soul don't rise older. You might be as youthful when you believe your subconscious mind never grows older. It's classic, timeless, as well as almost endless. It's part of this worldwide mind that was not created, plus it won't ever perish. Endurance, kindness, honesty, humility, fantastic will, serenity, stability, and brotherly love are qualities and attributes that never get old. In the event you still build those qualities on this plane of life, then you can consistently stay youthful in the soul.

Truth

Knowledge is the consciousness of the enormous noncircular powers on the mind and also the wisdom the way to correct to employ the following skills to direct the happiness and full existence. Make sure the memory never fades. It has to end up similar to a parachute that's not any great except if it opens upward.

10 productivity pointers to help you achieve your aims

Each one of us is talented the same 24 hours daily. It is the method that utilize those hours, even although, making all of the gaps, and that's precisely why executing some essential productiveness hints may create a significant change.

If you think like a lot of people, attaining the height of success will be difficult for you. This is the reason I am discussing my ten most useful productivity-boosting hints that is not complicated for one to execute now.

1) make use of the "twist it after" rule

The "touch it" rule states that you need to finish a job or job from beginning to complete the first time, which you simply feel it in the place of starting a task and allow it to end in a subsequent moment. Should you have the ability to devote to after this principle, it'll take away most chances for procrastination straight out from this gate.

2.) compose it away

If you have your own "to-do checklist" in a laptop, on the calendar, or in a mobile phone, composing the activities which you want to accomplish is a superior means to maintain your self-organized in addition to an excellent approach to be much more efficient too. There is only a thing about writing a set of activities that leaves someone more inspired to accomplish these and scrape them from the record by one. If a to-do set is on the mind, it's hardly over just something to stress. After a to-do set is composed, nevertheless, it turns into an idea that needs to be carried out.

3) establish modest targets

Goal-setting is just one of the most potent procedures for aiding an individual to accomplish their long-term goal. But, goal-setting may be used to assist you in reaching short-term goals and increasing your daily productivity too. Using dividing up a massive project into lots of bits and establishing "tiny objects" to finish those bits just by you, you can also benefit from these motivation-boosting added benefits of both goal-setting and utilize these to grow your productivity significantly.

4) approach ahead

Just before you close from work every day, prepare in advance by putting together your to-do set for that future moment. Planning the very next day's job inside this method gives you the ability to read the mind beforehand time to get the second day's job and enables one to dip directly to your to-do set as soon as the workday starts.

5) do not more than commit

Nothing surpasses your productivity, really like biting more than you can chew. Overcommitting to more excellent work when you might be competent to accomplish directs stress upon stress -- that could help it become tough to finish any job in the slightest. Although you do not desire to offer yourself short around the total amount of duty you may end in a specific period, you want to stay away from accepting significantly more than one could manage. It has a delicate balance, however, a significant someone to see if you are interested in being productive.

6) cease attempting to multi-task

While multi-tasking might appear to be a simple means to improve and enhance your productivity, if you are not multi-tasking properly, it inclines to wind up carrying out the specific contrary intent. At any time, you divide your focus between various endeavors, either the productivity and also the level of work are guaranteed to undergo. As an alternative of multitasking, provide 1 undertaking your entire care until it's done before continuing towards the following.

7) start with your hardest task

If you have the ability to full your difficult task out from this gate, so you're able to keep daily understanding the worst is right for you in the place of spending your afternoon stressing of an activity which you're dreading. Because too much stress will have a bad effect on your productivity, so first taking care of the hardest job in your to-do checklist can be an efficient approach to become more productive.

8) ascertain after you are most powerful

A lot of people are in their productive in the early morning. Others, however, could do their best work at night time or in the day time. Determine when you are most productive and utilize those periods with their entire benefit.

9) lessen interruptions

These days, we live in a world that provides one up disturbance and diversion after one opposite. In the event you are interested in being as successful as you can. Thus, it truly is important to get as a number of those interruptions as you possibly can. Close off yourself at a space and -- even if you're competent -- leave your cellphone in a separate area. Simply take all these steps that you can to shut yourself off of the surface world to ensure all that will be left is that you and also the task that has to be done.

10) establish time-limits

Few matters are somewhat more reaching compared to only deadlines. Also, you can benefit from putting practical, nonjudgmental time constraints onto the activities that you want to finish. Should you find it possible to take care of these time constraints together with the severity which you'd take care of a formal deadline afterwards, your productivity is sure to increase.

5 guidelines to produce the fantastic mindset for good results

Success isn't an event that you just attend to; it is a method of life span. In the event you wish to perform fantastic items, dedication has to be revealed in whatever you do.

So, no matter what it is that you wish to do, your path to success begins when you embrace the right mindset.

Listed below are just 5 ideas to create the perfect mindset for achievements.

1. Establish what success approaches

The very first measure of building a mindset for achievement would always be to specify exactly what this means to ensure success.

Putting targets for yourself makes it to be easier to think of an idea that will help you accomplish your dreams, and also certainly will inspire one to hold out this program.

Also, it provides you with a standard by which you measure your progress and adapt to your strategy. You need to, therefore, specify livelihood or life targets and think of the thing you have to do to reach them.

Try to take clever decisions in every part of the life which you desire to modify.

Also, make short every week, so which makes sure to align together along with your broader goals.

In case you have difficulty deciding where to begin, take a look at my target's quick-start master-class that will assist you in placing and reaching some objective.

2. Remain in touch together with your instinct

The 2nd measure to building a mindset for good results would always be to remain in contact with your instinct.

Some suppose that success entails making determined decisions based on general information. At the same time that you need to make an effort and be empirical as possible; these kinds of info aren't always offered.

Nothing your specific course, you will probably need to earn a decision sooner or later throughout your own life where there isn't any calculable reply.

This circumstance, you have to find a way to follow your instinct. While it isn't just an ideal supply of advice, our intuitions can usually straighten out problems quicker compared to conscious notion might.

This will enable one to make critical choices in complicated scenarios.

3. Continue to keep a positive frame of mind.

Never underestimate the worth of having a confident mindset towards achieving your goals.

Whatever the route you follow could be simple to become frustrated by temporary setbacks or failures to attain specific targets.

Favorable contemplating entails discovering those drawbacks, learning chances. This also causes it to be less challenging to overcome small failures and keep making attempts towards achieving your goals.

Favorable thinking also tend to cause you to a much pleasant man to be accessible, permitting one to draw attention from many others who can assist you in with the issue at hand.

4. Require action

You want to put your thoughts to actions. Besides favorable notions, a mindset for achievement additionally necessitates the belief to succeed.

Whenever you're thinking about your goals or barriers that stop you from achieving them, you ought to have the ability to recognize specific activities you may simply take in reply.

The faster you move a notion or motivation to functional activity, the simpler it's going to be to earn advancement towards your targets probably.

5. Take entire obligation

A mindset geared towards success entails having the capability to take accountability for everything you need to do if wrong or right.

Should you make a mistak, somebody, together with your course, getting responsibility enables you to comprise the damage and conserve your standing? Additionally, it motivates one to take into consideration how you might prevent that error later on.

Furthermore, in case you reach something, you've got to file for responsibility because of this. Just then can realize that which you could certainly do, along with encouraging you in your course for victory.

Chapter nine

What exactly is forgiveness?

Psychologists usually specify bias as a conscious, willful decision to discharge emotions of bitterness or vengeance towards an individual or staff who have wronged you, whether or not they deserve your forgiveness.

As significant as determining correctly what forgiveness is, however, is comprehending what validity is not. Pros who teach or study bias say that that as soon as you forgive, you don't shine over or refuse the seriousness of crime contrary to you personally. Forgiveness doesn't mean, nor does this suggest condoning or excusing offenses. Though bias might help mend a relationship, it will not induce one to collaborate with whoever disturbs you personally or discharge them out of legal responsibility.

Instead, bias gives the forgiver peace of mind and also frees them from irreparable rage. While there's a disagreement over the authentic preference demands positive opinions regarding the offender, professionals concur that it involves letting go of profoundly held grudges. If that's the manner, it empowers one to comprehend that the annoyance you've suffered without even enabling this pain set you personally, permitting one to recover and continue to move forward with your life.

The bible's response

Forgiveness is the action of pardoning a person who have wronged you. From the bible, the Greek phrase translated "validity" practically signifies "to go," as if an individual doesn't require cost for debt. Jesus employed this contrast after he educated his followers to pray: "forgive us all our sins, because we also forgive everyone else who's in our debt " (Luke 11:4) similarly, in their parable of the unmerciful servant, Jesus equated bias with depositing debt. --Matthew 18:23-35.

Forgiveness is complete when we let go of the bitterness and offer any claim to be paid to your harm or reduction we've endured. The bible instructs that unselfish love is that the cornerstone for authentic bias, because adore "doesn't due to this harm " --1 Corinthians 13: 5, 4.

What validity doesn't imply

You are condoning the crime. The bible truly condemns people that assert evil deeds are benign or okay. --Isaiah 5: 20.

Asserted, the crime indeed not transpire. God forgave king David of sins that were serious. However, he didn't defend David from the consequences. God had David's sins listed. Therefore, they are recalled now. --two Samuel 12: 9-13.

You are letting other people benefit from you. Suppose, as an example, for you to advance cash for somebody. However, the wastes it after which are not able to reimburse you since he'd sworn. He's quite respectful and apologizes for your requirements. You might opt to forgive him and not hold grudges, but perhaps not forgetting the thing with him and maybe even trapping the credit card debt directly. But you may also opt not to charge him some extra cash. --psalm 37:21; proverbs 14:15; 22:3; Galatians 6:7.

They are pardoned without a legal foundation. God doesn't forgive individuals that are guilty of deliberate, malicious sin and that won't admit their problems, alter their manners, and also confer with people that they will have harm. (proverbs 28:13; acts 26:20; Hebrews 10:26) such unrepentant ones eventually become god's enemies," also that he doesn't need us to forgive people that he's not whined. --psalm 139:21, 2-2.

Imagine you're the casualty of a cruel mistreatment by somebody who won't apologize or admit from that which exactly he gets ever done? The bible says: "let go of rage and also leave anger" (psalm 37:8) while perhaps not excusing the mistake, you may refuse to be overcome with wrath. Trust that god will attract someone to account. (Hebrews 10:30," 31) you may take comfort in realizing that god will deliver some while after we no longer sense that the profound ache or harm which will lead us today. -- Isaiah 65:17; revelation 21:4.

Forgiving each perceived minor. Sometimes, as opposed to pardoning a so-called offender, then we all can need to acknowledge we had no legal reason because of staying offended at the very first location. The bible states: "don't hesitate to take crime, because of the shooting of crime is that the marker of an idiot " --Ecclesiastes 7:9, footnote.

The way you can forgive somebody

Recall what validity will involve. You're not condoning the incorrect or behaving like it not occurred --you're only allowed it move.

Understands the advantages of forgiveness. Letting go of bitterness and anger can give you peace, strengthen your wellbeing, and elevate your contentment. (proverbs 14:30; Matthew 5:9) much more significant, while other people are still integral to getting god's forgiveness to your sins. --Matthew 6: 14, 15.

Be careful. We all are imperfect. (James 3:2) as we love being bemused, we ought to also forgive the errors of the others. --Matthew 7:12.

Be sensible. If we possess a slight cause for criticism, we could employ the bible's counselor: "continue setting up with just one " --Colossians 3: 13.

Act fast. Always make attempt to forgive anyone who has wronged you instead of bearing grudges. --Ephesians 4: 26, 27.

Forgiveness is very important

Wow!

The terms will be used 5 to 8 days from the new church on your own. It is demonstrably an essential idea into god the father. And likely will come as no real surprise for a lot you. However, only how long can we devote considering forgiveness--and placing it right into training?

The subject had been motivated with my warrior's recent article about precisely what this has to become a servant of Christ. As believers in Jesus, we're his brothers --along with his buddies. Just from god's view are those maybe not opposing realities. John 15:15 describes people while god the father's pals, yet, in the prior verse, Jesus educates teaches us that if we like him; we'll continue to keep his orders.

The way you can forgive somebody that has damage you in 10 measures

Forgiving others is important for one to develop spiritually. Your encounter with a person that has hurt you personally, while debilitating, is nothing more significant a feeling or sense that you simply take on. All these notions of bitterness, rage, and hate reflect sluggish, painful energies that'll disempower you when you keep letting those thoughts occupy your mind. If you were able to publish, then you would understand more serenity.

Here i discuss just how to forgive somebody who has hurt you personally in 10 steps:

Measure 1: proceed on the following act

Your previous heritage and of all your harms are no longer here. Do not let them function in your mind, muddying your moments. Your own life is much similar to a drama with different actions. A number of the personalities that input have quick functions to perform others, far more substantial. Many are villains, yet many others are all good guys. However, most of these are essential; in any other case, they'd not be from the play. Embrace all of them, and continue with your next step

Measure 2.: reconnect to spirit

Adopt a new arrangement on your own at all times and remain attached with spirit even if it sounds as the most difficult action to take. In the event you take care of so, you can allow whatsoever amount of flawless balance your human body was intended to increase. Switch your nerves to god and invite spirit to move.

Your new arrangement with the truth which you have combined yourself with your personality together with your divine god connected self-love will start to exude higher energy of light and love. Wherever you proceed, the others are going to have the shine of your god-awareness. Also, disharmony and disease, and all mode of problems only won't flourish in your presence. Eventually become "a tool of peace," because St. Francis wants the very first type of the renowned prayer.

Measure 3: do not proceed into snooze furious

Nightly like I ramble off into slumber, I wholeheartedly won't apply this time to assess whatever I do not wish to get fortified at the hours. To make my subconscious mind remains calm. I always opt to impress my subconscious mind my thought of myself because being a divine founder in working together with the one account. I reiterate that I am, that I've put into my creativeness, also that I understand that my slumber is going to be controlled with my final awakening theory of myself. I'm calm, I'm happy, and I adore, and I also keep only people who think as I do close.

That is my everyday ritual, so always eschewing virtually any desire to go above any panic of unpleasantness myself may be requesting me to critique. I suppose the atmosphere within my own body of the I'm statements fulfilled, also that I am aware I'm letting myself be more programmed throughout sleep, the next day I grow to understand that I'm a completely free representative.

Measure 4: alter the concentrate from allergic the others into recognizing your self

Each time you are angry about the behavior of others, consider focusing your mind on something else to ease your distress. Alter your mental energy, allowing yourself to function with everything you are believe -- Permit only the knowledge as much as you can, without even letting others know of your feelings. Do not blame yourself! Simply allow the experience to unfold and then let yourself know that nobody has the power to force you to get uncomfortable without your consent, also that you are reluctant to give this ability to the individual at the moment.

Explain to yourself which you are ready to openly encounter your own emotions with no calling them "incorrect" or wanting to chase them off. In this manner, you have to make a change to self-mastery. It is vital to skip blame, and also to skip your urge to know the different man; as an alternative, concentrate on comprehending yourself.

By accepting on how you choose to answer anyone or anything, you are aligning yourself with all the gorgeous dancing of your life. By simply altering the direction that you decide to comprehend the power others have above you and you also may understand a glowing new universe of infinite possibility for yourself. You're going to learn how to forgive immediately and give up any such thing.

Measure 5: stay away from notification people things to complete

Reject ideas and actions which demand to educate individuals that are perfectly competent of earning their particular decisions, everything things to complete. On your family, don't forget you usually do not possess a person. The poet Kahlil Gibran reminds you...

That is always correct. Simple fact dismiss any tendency to predominate all your relationships. Socialize as opposed to expound. Take care of yourself once you are possessing judgmental comments and determine at which self-attention happens to you. After you substitute for a possession mentality with you among making it possible for, you will start to see the authentic sanity of this on your life and other people's life. From that minute, you will be without any frustration together with people that do not act as per your ego-dominated anticipations.

Measure 6: know to let it go and end up like H_2O

As opposed to trying to control by force, end just like water flow everywhere, there is an introduction. Soften your challenging advantages by becoming more self-indulgent of other remarks. Interfere significantly less, and replacement listening to telling and directing. Whenever a person provides you with their view, consider reacting together: "I have never believed this previously – thank you. I will give a thought to it."

Photograph yourself with the exact traits as plain water. Permit your gentle, feeble, yielding, liquid to input regions at which you were excluded. As a result, your tendency to be sound and tricky. Flow lightly in the lifestyles of people with whom you're feeling conflicted: photograph your self-inputting their inner selves, visiting most likely for initially, they're undergoing. Maintain this picture of your personality just as lightly coursing water, also see the way your relationships with each other is different.

Measure 7: require responsibility for the section

Eliminating attribute does not means to stop delegating accountability to anybody else to whatever you are having. Additionally, it ensures you're eager to mention, "I don't know the reason why I believe that this manner why I have this ailment why I have been, or I had this collision, however, I am eager to express with no remorse or bitterness I loved it. I am living together with, and I will be accountable to get with it in my own entire life."

Should you choose accountability for getting the expertise, then you have a possibility to be responsible for eliminating learning out of this. In the event, you are in absolute modest (most likely as yet not known) manner in charge of this constipation headache or depressing sense. You may choose to try to take it off or find what its communication is right for you. If, on the opposite side, somebody or somebody different is still responsible for the mind, then naturally, you are going to need to wait patiently till they shift that you secure much better. And that's not likely to happen. This means you move house without a and therefore are abandoned without a serenity is genuinely around the opposite hand of this coin.

Measure 8: permit proceed of resentments

What can cause aggravation and rage soon after having a dare? The generic answer is laundry checklist detailing why one other man was erroneous and illogically and they behaved, finishing with something similar,

"I have the right to be angry if my [kid, mother-in-law, ex-husband, supervisor, or even whomever you believe about] talks to me without respect!"

However, in case you are curious about living a Tao-filled life, you must stop making this kind of considerations. Resentments do not originate out of the behavior of another party within an altercation. In essence, they live and flourish as you are reluctant to finish this altercation having a feeling of kindness, appreciation, along with true forgiveness. Since Lao-tzu states:

When most of the crying, yelling, and threatening sentences are made, that the moment for serene has come. Bear in mind that no storm continues indefinitely, which concealed inside are seeds of tranquility.

That was a period for bitterness, along with also a period for peace.

Measure 9: be kind rather than suitable

There's a Chinese proverb that says," whoever seeks revenge should dig two graves", same thing is what am saying: resentments will damage you.

The planet is only the manner it is. Those who are acting "poorly" from the earth do precisely what they genuinely are said to do. You may approach it in just about any manner which you pick. If you should be full of anger concerning most of those "problems," you're only one more one, which leads towards the contamination of rage. As an alternative, don't forget that you have nothing to gain when you seek revenge on anyone that wrongs you.

Try to foresee if a person states something for you, which you find offensive. Instead of opting for bitterness, figure out how to not let it get to you and react together with all kindness. You're prepared to openly ship the high, speedier energies of love, calmness, happiness, forgiveness, and service because the answer whatever happens your way. You can do so to yourself. You'd preferably be sort than just right.

Measure 10: exercise supplying

When in an argument or disagreements, clinic giving in the place of just taking until you depart. Giving calls for leaving the self. Once it desires to triumph and also reveal its excellence by staying disrespectful, your Tao nature wishes to be at peace and dwell in harmony. You can lower your leisure period to nearly zero if your clinic this process:

The significance of forgiveness

Defining forgiveness during the rear doorway:

To forgive does not mean you should condone being wronged.

He was achieving a location of authentic enlightenment. Will be perhaps not on you picking out what somebody else did is beautiful when it had been not.

Giving does perhaps not imply you must neglect (is that possible?).

What validity is: eliminating the negativity, which leads to harm by enabling go of emotional bags.

Why must we forgive?

Even though it may seem really reassuring or powerfully publishing to be forgiven, create no mistake: we don't overlook to its other man; we all forgive to get ourselves!

We forgive people who have wronged us to ensure our growth and enjoyment as soon as we continue to damage, discomfort, bitterness, and rage that it hurts us much higher than it hurts the culprit.

Forgiveness motivates us to dwell at the existing. Bearing grudges keeps us alive previously and overlooking now's magnificence.

Forgiveness enables us to go ahead with no anger or contempt or trying revenge.

As Confucius mentioned regarding resurrection," just before you set out on the journey of revenge, dig two graves." that applies up into this soul of rage, supporting the urge to have payback just as far concerning revival itself. Even if it's the case that you didn't know when you looked for revenge, then holding to a rage delivers down you.

Forgiveness enables us to recover personal power. Our rage, sorrow, hatred, or bitterness towards somebody usually means that we're quitting our control into this individual. Visualize a string all around your neck, then held with the person that wronged you. And soon you may forgive, you won't violate that string, and also the individual will nonetheless have a weak grip over you.

Forgiveness enhances and heals your physical and mental wellness. The devices of this human anatomy answer unwanted emotions, impacting the immune process in a way that may blow off your mind. Releasing these emotions can be wise.

Forgiveness accomplishes the cobwebs. Therefore, that you may observe the beautiful back again. After you forgive, you are going to have the ability to determine most of the constructive qualities at the man or woman who have wronged you -- qualities you adored --also enables one to accept them entirely, all simple, and also have an opportunity in a long-term, wholesome relationship.

When if we forgive?

After the hassle of carrying on into this wrongdoing from the earlier has been accompanying you into the long run, you own a decision. Be let it move.

The way to forgive?

If you're in a relationship, you would like to mend and keep; an acute and adoring conversation will be to be able.

Simply take your time to express your rage and hurt.

Wait patiently until you're reasonably sure that your spouse isn't going to replicate the treacherous action (i.e., he/she guesses that the wrong-doing, truly really wants to earn restitution, also vows not to replicate the blunder).

Tell him or her the way you are feeling (use "I" statements). "I believe damage / masked / fearful / stressed / grief-stricken etc.."

Ask issues which you have replied. This is a time for the whole revelation to your spouse. You've got the right to understand everything it's that you would like to follow.

Establish new bounds and connection.

Explain that you're picking to forgive.

In case, the damage happened in a previous relationship, and also you can't appear to move from under the rage, bitterness, or frustration it caused, and then your course of action will soon be an inside 1.

You may speak with a close friend or lifestyle mentor to talk your bias or compose out it in a diary.

Be certain you know what your emotions are and state them.

Put yourself in someone else shoes. As hard as that might be, even looking to comprehend just why she or he disturbs you, along with also your relationship, is quite crucial. (recognizing will not imply condoning but is a measure to for giving.)

Forgive to the donation to what occurred.

Leave that previously.

Locate the wonder on your life.

Forgiveness isn't only meant for lovers. We could all come across revived freshness inside our relationships when we can learn how to forgive. A lot of men and women locate their bonds to parents or siblings that have been restored and fortified. Discord using a neighbor or co-worker might be treated.

5 approaches to for giving the others

Communicate your self

When considering how to forgive somebody, it might or might not help express your feelings into one other individual. In case the relationship is significant for your requirements personally, and also you may love to keep it up. It can be helpful if you share with the individual man -- from English terminology --just how the activities influenced you (view this informative article about how to battle resolution for hints). In case the man or woman is no longer a part of your life if you'd like to take the relationship, or in case you might have cause to think that matters will probably become worse in the fact that you deal with the specific situation rightly. You might only need to compose a letter and then rip this up (or burn off it) and then go ahead. It may help put your emotions into phrases as a piece of allowing proceed.

People do not know you've to inform them forgiveness is higher for you than to one other individual.

Locate your favorable

Keeping a journal concerning a circumstance at which you were hurt or wronged might assist you to approach what happened and proceed ahead; yet, the direction that you write concerning it and also exactly what you opt to give attention to may make a big difference about how simple it gets to be forgiven. Research have shown that journaling concerning the advantages you have obtained out of an adverse scenario --instead of focusing on the emotions you've enclosing the big event or composing about something inconsequential may enable you to forgive and proceed more readily. So pick a pencil and begin tagging regarding the silver liner next occasion you locate somebody raining in your parade, or even maintain a continuous grateful diary and forgive a bit daily.

Cultivate empathy

Even though you do not need to concur with everything the other individual did to you, just focus on how best to forgive, often it will help you to put yourself at one other man's sneakers. Research have shown that compassion, especially for guys, is correlated with bias, also may make the procedure simpler. Rather than visiting them, "the enemy," attempt to comprehend precisely the variables which they had been coping with all the are heading via an extraordinarily tough period in their life? Have you ever made significant faults? Attempt to bear in mind that the other man's good qualities, so assume their motives are perhaps not to intentionally upset or wrong you (except you've got clear signs differently), and you also may discover that it's easier to forgive.

Guard yourself and continue ahead

You probably have heard of the expression: "1st time, shame for you; next time, shame." sometimes it truly is tough to forgive if you believe forgiveness leaves one receptive to prospective repetitions of the exact lousy therapy. It is necessary to realize that bias isn't the very same as condoning the offending actions, which is okay (and occasionally critical) to comprise tailor-made strategies for your long run as a portion of your mediation procedure.

For instance, if you have a co-worker that always appreciate your ideas, belittles you at the front of this bunch, or even gossips about your personal life, such bad behavior can be hard to forgive. But, you're able to create a strategy to deal with the act with individual funds, proceed to a different section, or swap tasks to escape from the unwanted circumstance.

Get assistance if you want

Occasionally it can be hard to forget the past and forgive, especially in a situation where the effect of the wrong done on you is traumatic or continuing. If you are having issues understanding just how exactly to forgive somebody who's wronged you at a substantial method, you may have superior accomplishment dealing together with a therapist who will be able to allow you to sort out your emotions onto the deeper degree and also support you in getting through the procedure.

Chapter ten

Take out mental cubes employing the subconscious

Subconscious blocks

Do you like you keep finding yourself in the same position over and over again?

Does this grab you off guard each moment?

A particular kind of relationship? Awful failures minutes before victory? Consistently attracting precisely, the same type of family members?

Even though enormous sums of work in the area to alter those scenarios, they merely. Keep. She is taking place.

If it seems comfortable, you may be having an unconscious block. Meaning your subconscious mind has made a type of barrier to shelter you from something it things will harm you.

Fortunately for you, you'll find ways it's possible to eliminate those cubes through sub-conscious mind prep.

Paradoxically, that is ideal! Now you can eliminate your subconscious cubes!

Regardless of what they're or who is the miscreant for placing them just are aware that it is achievable.

The power of the unconscious mind

Just before we enter the nitty-gritty of manipulating the subconscious mind, let us take a look at the power it retains.

The way your subconscious mind is programmed, straight influences your "computerized" or profoundly related action, i.e., that the things which you simply do with no knowingly hoping to.

The sub conscious mind may also have a grip on your emotions by activating the release of brain compounds that excite first reactions.

• you decide that you will return to school and complete your education. First, you will start having doubts, so in reality, you simply conjure every potential explanation regarding the reasons you'd not succeed and also don't follow along with your plans.

That is why behind committing up?

Can it be since the temptation had been too fantastic?

No.

The voice which recommends you to consume only a tiny parcel of chocolate also questions your capacity to ensure success is not you committing to temptation, however, also your subconscious programming is taking part in and around on mind.

That distress or resistance to improve would be your subconscious block.

Actions to eliminate misaligned cubes

1. Know your emotions

Let us begin on this specific exercise. I would like one to jot the very first idea that pops up in the mind when you make these phrases.

Do not rationalize them. Simply run together with all the exact first thing that comes to mind. I will let you know after you finish the workout:

Rich men and women

Currency

Good results

Really like

How can you solve it?

Can you say, "successful people are manipulative and evil?" or perhaps you moved straight back into this adage..."money may be the origin of evil." in case your idea routines proved to become like that which i only said, then those beliefs could be stopping you from achieving authentic prosperity.

Also, you may have claimed that abundant persons... Are blessed since these certainly were born with silver spoons in their mouths" this form of opinion retains you believing that victory is merely the consequence of fortune or perhaps a birth afforded to your select couple. It disturbs you by visiting you may create your own life whatever that you would like to buy to become.

You view it requires the same quantity of attempt to feel that you're doomed to poverty, even because it will help to find yourself blessed with wealth. Both final results (poverty and wealth) would be the thought on one's mind.

Negative ideas boost deficiency, lack, dread, and maybe even procrastination.

positive ideas, on the other hand, return wealth, an excitement for action, and life.

2. Reflect

wealthy parents told me, "money will not grow on bushes " or maybe "I am not made of money...cash's challenging to find."

A lot people don't comprehend that a large part of things which our parents/guardians' thought was predicated in their very own self-limiting customs. They've experienced their subconscious blockages, which were indeed not treated. They may have invited one to receive yourself a stable work that has a fantastic 401k program, if your actual fire may have already been a livelihood in songs or even perhaps artwork.

Exactly what your father and mother advised you along with also your capacity to succeed has improved your subconscious and conscious mind.

Stop letting yourself become programmed!

It is your life, therefore live it!

3. Listen on your self-talk, feelings, & emotions

What kind of emotions does one have when they are making a purchase in the supermarket or any time you are making any form of expenses? Are you crazy? Have you been upset? Is it true that the considered money departing you create you truly feel uncomfortable?

If that's the case, this is possibly the reason why prosperity is not circulating during your own life.

That applies in different areas, too, such as friendships and relationships. If you meet up with a new person, while it is platonic or maybe romantic, are you initially suspicious?

Asking yourself who they are and what they want from you?

After things start going well using somebody else, can you wind up waiting to get an "inescapable" struggle along with break?

Be exceptionally mindful of the ideas that goes through your mind and stop you every time you grab yourself staying unwanted. At another step, you are going to discover how-to

4. Picture

Take away your unconscious blockages by utilizing visualization.

Once you have tracked your ideas and responses to words such as cash, accomplishment, and maybe even adore, you may utilize visualization to improve them.

Generate an accurate mental picture of your goal and also the person you want to be. Shut your eyes and picture your ends. When it truly is fiscal liberty which you would like afterward, visit it, sense it, then make sure it. When it truly is like, the exact very same policies apply. The truth is that no matter what your aim is, possibly, you only have to validate and imagine

The subconscious mind does not understand the gap between reality and fantasy. Thus, the further you imagine it, the more you'll deceive it in believing its true.

Continue working in those ways.

Create sure they are daily clinics.

Allow these to be the first thing that you do in the daytime and also the last thing you do at night.

Be persistent, stubborn, and also you may take out your subconscious cubes.

5 best methods to remove and contain your hidden blocks to achievement

Discover your own subconscious mind's education about currency

Let us focus on just a tiny bit of physical exercise. I need some to give immediate answers to these following words. Do not even presume relating to these. Simply expect that the first thing that comes to mind. I will let you know after you finish the workout:

Rich men and women

Currency

Success

Financial freedom

How can you solve it? Can you say that, "successful people... Have been snobs." or "dollars... Will not grow on bushes." if you did, then this will inform you have damaging unconscious beliefs that can be keeping you again.

You may have said, "successful individuals are blessed." while this may seem to be an optimistic statement, it may perhaps not be. If you don't commonly think about yourself as someone with a great deal of luck, then subsequently, your subconscious mind will stop you from turning out to be loaded.

Associated: the best way to conquer allergic beliefs

2. Allergic on what's children told you personally

Maybe you're a normal pupil, and you noticed, "you are not likely to succeed if you continue moving with one of these sorts of grades!" or "you're so lazy! You won't ever amount to something in your life in case you never wake fully up and do something.

What your parents advised you concerning yourself along with also your capacity to succeed has improved your subconscious and conscious mind.

Also, if you heard announcements such as "you need to spare for a wet afternoon," or even "what can you presume I am manufactured from...funds?" subsequently, your father and mother told you the funds are are hard to generate.

If they think that the odds are, you also do, even if it's the case that you never consciously understand it.

Associated: the way to get a favorable money mindset

3. Monitor your self-talk, feelings, & emotions

How can you believe as if you are paying bills? Have you got a sinking sensation of all the money that's is going outside? Or does one genuinely feel grateful you have dollars to pay for invoices? After you attend the retail store, can you state, "I cannot afford this" or even "if I can win the lottery"

The way you talk to yourself around money will contribute in making you get the money. Be mindful of the ideas which move through the mind and stop yourself every single time you grab yourself staying unwanted.

4. Make use of affirmations and visualization

After number three, even once you understand that the negative thoughts which go through your mind, utilize visualization and adjectives to shift it out automatically.

Make positive statement regarding success and money and also replicate them over. Wear them poster boards close to your home and start looking at these regularly. Additionally, shut your eyes and picture your ends. Watch yourself into your ideal livelihood or perhaps a happy relationship. Feel it. Watch it. Become it.

The subconscious mind does not understand the gap between reality and fantasy. Thus, the further you imagine it, the more you'll deceive it into believing its true.

5. Program your unconscious mind with hypnosis.

Hypnosis is creepy and strange. It keeps your brain calm so that the waves so that you're more receptive to hints as well as Jelqing. Therefore, if you've noticed that your mom and dad taught you that "money is the root of all evil" effectively, you do a bit re programming asap.

There are many sites online where you can download mp3 tapes on hypnosis. The further you employ hypnosis, the more the much more you'll eliminate all of the programming's you personally, the more parents, your parents, and also society also have instilled in your subconscious. Believe me, it works.

4 essential methods to erase sub-conscious negativity

Rewriting negative sub-conscious programs

As stated before, your subconscious mind is similar to a computer's hard disk. And only like individuals can disable and place new applications into a challenging ride, then we can encode data to the subconscious mind.

Chapter eleven

The act of being happy

The best way to be joyful: 1-5 methods to be happier

We often ask questions, "what can I do to increase my delights? "

I tell them there are a lot of things that you can do, yes. However, I have composed a novel on ways or things to do so you can be happy, at the tech era, "I regularly can just remember a couple of methods to utilize inside the present time. Thus, I decided to generate this comprehensive guide on the best way you can be joyful, based on science fiction. In the event you utilize those 2 to 3 techniques continuously; you are quite very likely to boost your private pleasure:

1. Learn the things to complete.

How can you suppose to construct the proper contentment skills for those who don't understand what you're fighting for from the beginning? This is the reason why it is beneficial to choose a quiz to research joys' strengths and flaws. Get a better understanding of this knowledge is typical about, and also know how to enhance your faults and construct your "contentment advantages."

2. Give yourself an assurance increase.

Why can you hassle growing your happiness if you did not consider you might succeed in it? You'd not. This is the reason why it is essential to advance your self-efficacy and show yourself which you can boost your happiness. The very optimal/optimally means to do so is by starting up with more natural abilities -- expertise such as gratitude or even prioritizing hanging out doing new issues. Obtain yourself a fast triumph, and you're going to be confident you can modify your own life.

3. Fuel your advancement in figuring out how to feel about yourself.

You would not learn mathematics to secure much better at cooking. And you'd not find some other terminology to shed weight. In order more joyful, you will pro earn far more development by emphasizing the relevant skills which are most closely connected to delights. During my exploration, the art that usually proves to be closely correlated to enjoyment would be a favorable self-view. Mastering how to feel great about yourself -- for example, by picturing your absolute best self, imagining your desirable features, or differentiating your strengths -- may go quite a method to boosting your happiness.

4. Produce balance and overcome burn-out.

How are you supposed to have the energy to be more joyful when you are stressed, drained, and unhappy out of your work? It'll be extremely tricky. Constructing new abilities, expertise which may help you're more joyful will devote some time and energy therefore that it's helpful to make a much better work-life balance.

5. Have the mind of an expansionist

An expansionist mindset gives the perception that we could alter ourselves. As soon as we create an expansion mindset for enjoyment, we consider we can change our pleasure. That is essential, as when we don't feel we will boost our happiness, we won't even stress to strive.

6. Ensure optimistic reminiscences.

Every part of our brains could be fortified throughout the training. When our brains have been great at recalling unwanted objects which transpire, it could help to fortify the aspects of the mind responsible for remembering real objects.

7. Locate those silver linings.

That which we encounter could be bummer if we opt to view it like that. However, while you look to find your silver lining or benefits in your daily life, you may as well be surprised to detect plenty of good. Continue training to boost the favorable and also reduces the unwanted to foster enjoyment. Additionally, this talent was connected to your better power to manage stress and be also resilient.

8. Check breaks out of societal networking.

Facebook has an unfortunate result on the contentment. From deciding to take a break from Facebook -- changing just how we utilize interpersonal media marketing -- we can increase our enjoyment.

9. Spend more intelligence for further enjoyment.

The best way we choose to spend money affects that which we may perform and the way that we are living in a way that impacts just how joyful we all have been. As soon as we select a fancy home or car or truck – things that do not give us much enjoyment -- we still do have significantly more income to expend adventures or even about gift ideas for good friends: cases which do give us joy.

10. Converse kindly.

We have been typing to other people, we believe about ourselves. We can do beautiful things for many people, be empathetic, or we could only take care of each other in regard, communication kindly as opposed to supposing the hardest.

11. Conclusion your unwanted styles of believing.

Let us face it, sometimes we are the ones making ourselves to be unhappy. We simply cannot quit considering how so wronged show our entire life did not prove even as we all expected. Painful idea procedures -- such as stressing, ruminating, self-judgment, along with dreading rejection only makes us unhappy and struggling to move ahead. As soon as you wind up thinking negatively, then pause and emphasize your thinking. With time, the human brain should be in a position to try so more readily by itself.

12. Come across clarity.

How can you maneuver your own life forward whenever that you never know that which you believe or you believe it? To eventually become happy, strive, and attain awareness of your own emotions; figure out what you are thinking and exactly what induced those emotions.

13. Know your worth.

When you start to research your worth, you will observe that you have understood all together what will make you happy. Nevertheless, you are only not performing this. In order to be happier, get crystal clear in your worth, therefore you may dwell your own life autonomously, by your principles and value.

14. Fork out focus into this great.

Surely, sometimes, daily life is not hard. However, by giving attention on this great, you also can grow over it and also be far resilient. As soon as you locate the nice, enjoy as soon as, also make it together to keep pleasure during the time of crisis. Or decide to try believing about some time in the long run when you are going to feel much better.

15. Take advantage of your creativity to make your life the way you want it to be.

Are you aware that your brain has a hard time differentiating among things that occur on your creativeness and issues that take place in your real life? Therefore, once you envision something even happiness -- your brain operates as though it is real. We can work with creativity to aid make contentment from the thin atmosphere and love our adventures.

The way to be joyful: 10 routines to enhance your regular

Day-to-day customs

1. Smile

You are inclined to smile when you are happy. However, it's a two-way street.

We laugh because we are happy, and also grinning induces the brain to produce dopamine, which causes us more joyful.

That does not mean that you have to go around with a phony smile plastered on your face all of the time. However, next time you feel like to crack a smile and determine what the results are. Or decide to try starting every morning with smiling at yourself in the mirror.

2. Exercise

Exercising is not merely for the human entire body. Regular exercise might help reduce stress, anxiety, and symptoms of melancholy while fostering self-esteem and enjoyment.

The right touch of bodily activity may earn a distinction. You do not possess to prepare to get a scale that a pond -- except if that is what helps to make you happy.

The secret isn't to overexert. Should you out of the blue throw into a rigorous regular, you are likely to end up defeated (and tender).

Contemplate these workout starters:

Have a stroll around the block every night after you have had dinner

Subscribe to get a newcomer's course in yoga or even Taichi.

Kick off your day with five moments of stretching. Following is a listing of stretches to secure you all started.

Remind yourself of some things you derive pleasure from. You appreciated, however, who's dropped by the wayside. Or tasks you usually desired to take to, for example, as golfing, bowling, or even dance.

3. Get enough sleep

However, much contemporary culture steers us to sleep; we are aware that sufficient rest is a vital or our good health, brain feature, and also emotional wellbeing.

Most adults want about 8 or 7 hours of sleep every day. In the event you realize that you are battling the desire to rest during daily or only generally really feel as though you are at a fog, then the own human body could be telling you how it takes more remainder.

Listed below are some ideas that will help you construct a better sleep pattern:

Take note of how many hours of sleep that you get every evening and how rested you feel. After having a week, then you still ought to get a more excellent idea the way you do.

Go to bed and wake up at the same time every evening.

Reserve the summertime as a silent moment. Have a bathroom, examine, or perform some soothing. Stay away from over drinking and eating.

Keep your bedroom dark, cold, and silent.

Buy a comfortable bed.

If you want to rest, attempt and restrict it to 20 minutes.

If you often find it hard to sleep, speak with your physician. You can possess a snooze ailment demanding treatment method.

4. Eat mood in mind

You know the type of food you eat has an effect on your general wellbeing. However, some food items may also affect the state of your mind.

For example:

Carbs discharge dopamine; a hormone that makes you feel good. Maintain low level of carbohydrates -- food items full of starch and sugar to the very least, since energy spike is brief and you're going to crash. Intricate carbohydrates, like veggies legumes, and whole grains, are somewhat all better.

Lean poultry, meat, legumes, and milk are packed with protein. These foods give dopamine and also norepinephrine that raises energy and focus.

Processed or deep-fried foods tend to make you feel down. Thus, we will jump dishes.

Start with producing one more excellent meal option daily.

For instance, take Greek yogurts for breakfast instead of pastry. You are going to meet your teeth, however, and also the nourishment may assist you to avert a mid-morning energy wreck. Consider including a new diet in your menu every week.

5. Be thankful

Only being thankful could provide your disposition with an enormous enhance, one of the additional positive aspects. For instance, research has shown that training dependence could have no small effect on emotions of happiness and hope.

Start your day by realising one thing you are thankful for. You certainly can do so as you are cleaning your teeth or only awaiting this snoozed alert to set off.

When you kick off your daily activity, attempt and maintain a watch outside for lovely items on your life. sometimes it feels good to know that someone loves you or that you are getting a promotion at work

However, they are also able to be small matters, these as a co-worker who gave you that a cup of java or perhaps the neighbor that dared to you personally. Probably even only the heat of sunlight in the skin.

Using a tiny bit of practice, you can also become mindful of each of the beneficial things you have.

6. Provide a glow

Research have shown that displaying acts of kindness can help you sense more fulfilled.

Giving out a pure glow is a fast, simple means to enhance a person's day while supplying your happiness to arise.

Get the individual's attention and say it with a smile on your face so that they understand your intent. You may be taken aback by just how it gets you experience.

If you want to compliment or admire someone's appearance, be sure you do it respectfully. Below are a few suggestions to secure you all started.

7. Breathe calmly

You are stressed, and your shoulders are tight, so and you are also feeling like you might "shed it" we are all aware that experiencing.

Instinct will let you know to choose quite a long-time deep breath to calm yourself down.

Figuring out, this intuition is a great

One particular. As stated by Harvard wellbeing, heavy breathing exercises help

Lessen stress.

Next time you truly feel stressed or sarcastic, perform using these ways:

Close your eyes, try to picture some joyful memory or gorgeous location.

Just take a slow, deep breath through your nose.

Gently breathe through your mouth or nose.

Repeat this it many times, before you begin to feel calm down again.

In case you are having a hard time breathing, so consider counting to 5 on mind together with every inhale and then exhale.

8. Acknowledge the sad seconds

A positive mindset is a great thing. However, bad stuffs happen to everyone. It truly is merely a part of everyday life.

In a situation where you receive bad news, don't let it ruin your mood. Pretend to be happy and keep a positive mindset.

Acknowledge the sensation of hopelessness, letting yourself encounter it to get an instant. After that, alter your attention on everything cause you to are feeling that this way and that which it may require to recoup.

Can a breathing exercise be of help? Or taking a walk? Discussing it over with somebody else?

Enable the minute move and care of yourself. Bear in mind, no person's content all of the moment; point.

9. Maintain a diary

A diary is a great way of keep record of the events that take place in your life assess your emotions, and also create ideas. And you also really don't need to become described as a literary genius or compose volumes to advantage.

It is often as easy as jotting down a few ideas before going to sleep. If placing particular vital things written down, which makes you nervous, then you may consistently fix it whenever you have completed it. It is what you do that matters.

Perhaps not sure things to accomplish with most of the current suspicions that wind up to the webpage? Our guidebook about composing your emotions will help you.

10. Confront stress head-on

Daily life is filled with stress. Also, it is hopeless to steer clear of most of them.

There is no requirement to. Stanford psychologist Kelly McGonigal claims that stress is not always detrimental, and also, we can alter our perspectives concerning its importance. Know more regarding the upside-down fear.

For many stress you cannot prevent, remind yourself that everybody else needs stress -- there is not any cause to consider it is about you. And odds are, you are more powerful than you think you are

Rather than letting yourself get overwhelmed with stress, attempt to attack the stressor head-on. This may signify tripping an embarrassing dialogue or placing in a few additional functions, however, the more quickly you handle this, the before your pet on your gut will begin to shrink.

Chapter twelve

Utilize your mind absolutely

Methods to train your brain to be positive

1. Celebrate your thoughts.

The very first place to begin is by detecting your mind -- also supposing it is only for 10 minutes. Due to the fact we are a monster of customs, you can see you have the same negative notions creeping in your mind. Are you concerned about an approaching journey? Are stressed outside operate? Are you crazy about the struggle you had with your better half?

As soon as you understand what conflicting ideas are. Bothering one of you should begin focusing on a method to fix the problem. For instance, if you have a misunderstanding with a co-worker then approach your supervisor with all the problem and get when it's possible to be transferred into a different section of the place of work in which there's no necessity to socialize using them too much better.

2. Scan to your three everyday advantages.

For you to have a sound sleep, you have to train your brain. Think about your daily life and think around three fantastic individual items that occurred for you daily. Whether it had been someone obtaining you a cup of java, a remarkably beautiful pond, or even getting a fresh consumer. The tiniest things, such as currently being paid off a comforter, with lunch with the elderly close friend, or also seeing with the furry friend roster round, are far somewhat more than just enough to force you to be happy.

The smaller things such as being paid out a glow, with lunch with the elderly close friend, or even seeing with the pet roster round, are far somewhat more than just enough to force you to get joyful.

3. Give someone a shout-out.

Gratitude is very important. Research has shown that showing appreciation may perform anything out of which makes you optimistic about the caked of coronary artery disorder. A gratitude diary is a great spot to commence. However, I have discovered that sharing your endings benefits you more.

It might be everything out of approving a colleague or employee for everyone their hard job, an instant grabbing up electronic mail having a buddy, equaling your barista, or even using a nightly talk including "what's the optimal portion of one's day now?" with your partner.

It can be a bit embarrassing from the start but believe me; you are going to feel great once you offer someone a shout-out.

4. Help others.

Whether it's assisting a swamped colleague onto an undertaking, helping someone pay their bill, then helping somebody in the office using an undertaking, keeping open a doorway, buying a stranger a cup of java, committing dollars, or some other kinds of act of kindness could boost enjoyment.

5. Familiarizing yourself with favorable men and women.

Considering that emotions are infectious, it merely is logical which you would wish to encircle yourself with positive minded men and women that encourage, empower, and inspire one personally, and perhaps not all of these Debbie downers and unfavorable Nancy's.

The power of positive thinking: your point of view on issues can change your life

The way to think positively

Predicated on several emotional evaluations, joyful men and women appear to get an excellent exceptional quality that allows them to live a far better life compared to normal.

Would you imagine everything? This is?

It is the caliber of optimism!

The optimal information for truth is the fact that it is a premium top quality. This means that you start having positive things in your life by thinking positively.

From the legislation cause and consequence, should you do and state what additional nutritious, happy individuals using positive perspectives do, and state, you'll quickly have precisely the same style, make the correct benefits, and relish precisely the exact experiences they perform.

Joyful people today uncover good from the planet

Optimists appear to have various methods of managing the entire world that place them aside in your regular.

To begin with, they maintain their minds focused only on their desire and also continue searching for ways to achieve it. They're clear regarding aims, and so they genuinely are convinced they will reach these sooner or later.

2nd, optimists search for what is sweet in most problems or issues. When things fail, as they tend to do, they still say, "that is fine!" then set about locating some item favorable in regard to the circumstance.

what we understand is this; if you're searching for something beneficial or good at an individual or scenario, you are going to believe it is consistent. And as you're hunting, you're going to be described as a positive and cheerful individual.

The power of good thinking

Optimists try to learn a lesson from every single setback or alteration. Instead of becoming angry and blaming someone else to get what's transpired, they just take command over their emotions by saying," "so what do I learn from that adventure?"

Resolve now to discover just how to create good thinking as well as also a favorable attitude on your own, individuals close to you, and even your life.

How can you prepare your mind to think positively?

Teaching your mind to think optimistically may be accomplished by implementing an original idea. The account gets ample bandwidth to focus on a single consideration at one moment; point. Whatever you need to do is maintain it dedicated to inspirational ideas, and soon you produce the exact kinds of nerve pathways which can be generated once you set a brand new custom.

Every time a drawback event happens, don't forget it's the answer that genuinely establishes the results. Consistently search for that positive lesson if such occasions occur.

Favorable affirmations are favorable phrases that may be replicated over and more to educate you on how you can get rid of unwanted ideas and create a pleasant frame of mind.

Also, I locate motivation from inspirational estimates, and messages must be somewhat helpful when seeking to drive optimistic ideas.

Decide to become joyful

Re solve from now. watch the cup of your life overflow unlike when it was empty.

Joyful men and women contribute thanks to many blessings in lifestyle as opposed to worrying or whining about what they don't need.

Have the best wish for people around you. A lot of people are respectable, straightforward and therefore are attempting to get the top that they understand just how exactly to. When you try to find something useful inside their voice and activities, you are always going to detect some stuff.

At length, try to be happy regardless of what the outcome may be.

Seeking the bright facet is the most essential when things fail.

Your favorable movements doing his thing

It is not difficult to be favorable if all is going according to plan. However, it can be once you come across sudden drawbacks and dilemmas, which you simply demonstrate yourself, and also the entire world over you personally, what type of mindset you have.

Methods to coach your sub-conscious mind for favorable considering

You are knowledgeable about this indisputable fact. You must remain good! Studies have shown that being optimistic enhances both bodily and mental wellness, and positivity fosters your inner vibration so that you're capable of showing precisely what exactly you'll want.

But it is not very easy to remain favorable once you come across sudden troubles or unwanted men and women. That is the reason you require smart tactics to instruct the human brain to remain favorable.

1. Sub-conscious re-training

It is important to be more concerning the very most effective modern methods for discovering and discharging the negativity you are carrying indoors. Beyond adventures, notable individuals in the youth could be kept at mind and the human body for decades, so yanking down you and reevaluate your possibility.

Exercises such as tapping and also neuro-linguistic programming can help you to get all these part on your own and build an even far more inviting and supporting belief-system (generating and strengthening new synapses (particularly on your adrenal gland).

Some people find hypnotherapy or meditation to be of help.

You can experiment together with numerous ways. However, the essential thing here is the fact that generating and keeping up a positive outlook frequently starts with confronting and enabling go of long-term consequences.

2. Give positivity to feel positivity

There is proof that kind behavior do not only make other people happy; nevertheless, they cause you to feel good too truly. Even only going for a time to accomplish some a little favor or simply helping a stranger can put you in a better state of mind, and also tear you from the unfavorable believing loop.

If you build the habit of doing something for a different man each time you feel down, stressed, or despairing, it is going to grow soon to be automatic. Also, unwanted durations will endure for shorter intervals.

3. Give attention to which can make you glad to be performed

Yes, one of the most efficient ways to prepare your brain. To remain confident is always to blatantly and turn your focus to matters which inspire happiness. It is truly a fantastic idea to devote some particular laptop to your specific pursuit, and then utilize it to list five this sort of matters daily.

Attempt to consider distinct classes as you do so. For example, interactions that allow you to be happy, parts of the earth close to you which you discover inspirational, and also facets of yourself which will enable you to feel joyful and positive truly. Once your thinking has been centered on happiness, you will fortify the neural pathways in the human brain and certainly will learn longer to become happier about like a consequence.

4. Appearance following the human anatomy

Our best studies show that what you drink and eat could have a big effect on your emotional condition, as will your way to sleep soundly and even your physical exercise. Consequently, if you'd like to become a much far better favorable thinker, have an excellent vital look in the manner in which you can care for the entire body and recognize prospective areas for advancement.

Diet can be a significant factor. Are you currently dieting on vitamins, minerals, and minerals nutrition? Can you differ your daily food ingestion to encourage much better wellbeing? There are set up links among vitamin deficiencies along with problems, including depression as well as anxiety.

Not getting up to 8 hours sleep daily can have a negative impact on your mindset and leave you unhappy. Since you tackle both the bodily sections of you personally with higher maintenance, the more mental and emotional components of you personally may react in variety.

5. Establish particular time to that which you adore

Together with all our job and societal responsibilities, it is truly simple to say we don't have enough time for those things people want. But without producing the distance at our own lives because of the most significant passions readily become gloomy and unwanted.

6. Turn negatives into positives

Best methods to re train your brain right into a favorable powerhouse

1. Celebrate your thoughts.

Supposing it's only to get 10 seconds. Later but you cannot fix a problem you do not understand. The moment you see the believing, you're going to learn the way to get started.

2. Select a mantra for your afternoon.

In the early hours, decide over the mantra. You'll see it softly on your own when you start your everyday life. Perhaps it's something as easy as "now is amazing" or even "I am a happy fellow." with a mantra is not only going to provide you with something beneficial to consider of but also it uses the time that your brain could likewise utilize unwanted notions.

3. Utilize a program.

In this digitalized modern society, there is a software for every task --for example, favorable believing. Look at these five meditation programs that will assist you in locating your inner relaxed.

4. Change a negative into a positive.

We all have a single idea that dominates our mind. To get several, it is that more 10 kilos we have been working tirelessly to eliminate. As an example, financing may weigh down us. Simply take that most crucial dilemma and transform it all in an affirmation. Rather than concentrating on additional weight, state into yourself, "I am wondering just how I'm." it won't create that pesky 10 lbs. return, however, nevertheless, it is going to supply you with self-confidence along with the drive.

5. Produce a gratitude list.

Time without number days, sit with a sheet of newspaper, and also develop with five things you are thankful for. May be the a/c on the own car that the ideal treatment for summertime heating? Are you reading an excellent publication? Contrary to popular belief, these items and much more are some things to be thankful for. Producing a mailing checklist may change your mood and also help keep you concentrated on the favorable in lifestyle.

Chapter thirteen

You are what you think you are

You might be everything you believe

Ralph waldo Emerson stated that, "you know exactly what you believe throughout the day " as a therapist," I have learnt how to show customers their notions significantly affect their moods and changing emotions, their own behavioral decisions, their self-confidence, the nutritious pitfalls that perform or are not accepted, and also their feelings of self-worth along with self-esteem in most areas of everyday life. Many wildly accepted ideas may have a weak and sustained effect. Here I talk about a number of these also learn more about the methods by which shifting people's ideas often leads to beneficial lifestyle modifications.

1. "I am afraid -- so I can't."

It is remarkable how fast things go "there is no use in believing or trying success may be gained." an exact smart and gifted client has been offered marketing inside of his company. Even though he required to go up the ladder, he maintained turning the ability simply because he was scared to talk into huge classes and understood that would be a portion of this project. I propounded a new theory built to modify his believing be fearful and also do it anyway. That made a distance for him to look at the idea the panic did not need to take a hold in his life. He is amenable to healing, facing, and coping, along with his fear rather than making decisions to stay clear of what amuses it. He moved on toast masters to know standard presenting and public talking competencies, also we role played them. we took a breath in and out to calm him down, directed vision to assume victory, and too positive self-talk to observe modest ways ahead. In essence, he had been competent enough to work throughout the panic and even take the promotion.

2. "I will never locate anything, anyone, higher yet; this really can be as good because it receives "

Countless women and men use this mindset to strained relationships and dead-end tasks. One client was at a long-term relationship and had been indeed not becoming her needs fulfilled. However, she had been scared; nobody better could come together, so she would not be okay when she was not in a relationship. This interpreted in to "so, I must settle" The new idea we adopted to use as solution, so I don't need to stay back, also that I don't need to visit again, even that I don't need to place a glass ceiling onto hos excellent stuff maybe" we focused around the specifications she stored for buddies that have been relationship, therefore that she would start to put up to the very same, broader criteria within her particular relationships. In case she would not invite her good friends to repay, why is she? This, focused on self-strengthening and increasing self-esteem, allowed her to get rid of that relationship. She remained solitary and uncovered that she would possibly be ok by her personal. The truth is that her entire life became fulfilling after she began to recover all of the things, she'd placed on the other side to adapt her partner.

3. "I left my bed. Today I must lie inside it."

Lots of cultures and families encourage this idea, particularly in elderly generations. Whatever you decide is accepted, you can not detract from this or even change your mind. To accomplish this is correlated with "quitting," fatigue," or even "failure," a person enrolled in therapy simply because he was legal counsel for nearly 30 years and loathed his livelihood. He picked it to his dad, that was likewise a lawyer. He realized right away nothing in regard to the task together along with his "truest self," but he devoted to law faculty and also afterward the business he sensed trapped. His new idea, "selecting to generate a shift is a symptom of strength and courage, which is my best to achieve that." he gave him consent to obey their very own interior intellect. Also, it did not take very long for him to appreciate that he wanted was to teach high school students. He assembled his guts, permit his spouses to buy him out of their business, discounted each of the naysayers, also to get its past couple of decades he's been instructing at a private college and hasn't ever been more joyful.

The essential power of the mind to grow that which you imagine

Your mind is a powerful thing, and also, the majority folks accept it as a right. We consider we're not accountable for that which we presume due to the fact that our minds appear to go in and out all day long. However, you might be a responsible charge of one's mind. Also, you eventually become precisely what you imagine. And the little kernel of the fact is that the trick power of their mind.

It is not a mystery in the slightest. Even the power is given to every individual, for example, you. And it's completely free.

"The trick" is you are exactly what you believe. You feel exactly what you believe. You may make your life that you need by simply finding the most suitable ideas.

Earl nightingale on "the strangest secret"

Back in 1956, earl nightingale composed "the strangest secret" within a try to show folks the power of their mind, the power of an idea. He stated, "you feel exactly what you consider all day."

Nightingale's came from napoleon hill's book, "think and grow rich," released in 1937.

For 75 years (and probably long before this), this uncomplicated "top secret" was taught to individuals across the globe. At least, the wisdom was around for people.

The way a power of this mind may operate to increase your lifetime

We have been animals of practice. We have tendency to adhere to the things we are taught by our parents or neighborhoods, our cities, and also the region of the planet from that we encounter for good or bad.

However, now we don't need to. We all have a mind of our own, with the capacity of picturing life exactly how we need to buy. We could say no or yes into the thousand decisions we all each encounter each day. Sometimes it is better to state no, obviously, or people might not receive anything whatsoever. However, the many prosperous folks say indeed alive all around. They've been given chances They consider they have the power to earn changes within their own lives. They're not scared to use new ideas to neglect.

Lots of their absolute most powerful companies reward individuals having the guts to decide to try new items, even should they neglect, as the matters people predict failures regularly develop into potent entities. Was your aware post it records turned into an error at first?

The way to make use of the power of one's mind

Start with imagining that your life is going the direction that you like it to. Create an image on mind and take into account this film all day. Think about it.

That you never need to teach a person. Have your very own silent confidence you may produce the movie on mind be realized.

You're going to start making distinct decisions in accord using your photograph. You'll require modest actions in the most suitable route.

Additionally, you will overcome challenges. Do not allow those challenges to prevent you. In the event you'd like the photograph of their life span, you would like loyal on the mind, you are going to make your life span gradually.

What are you got to get rid of? Close to your eyes and begin today.

You may end up exactly what you consider

Bible perspective

The very first two posts we've recorded in this department titled, "sanctification" and "mindset: being transformed by renewing your mind," all put the point for you personally demonstrating which it's the will of god on the daily life that you simply let him input you in sanctification method to ensure that he can entirely consecrate one to himself and start off to mildew, form, and change into the state image of his son Jesus Christ.

Inside this sanctification procedure, 1 of them the very first affairs you'll discover that the lord would like to accomplish together with you will always be to decide to try to put right thinking in the mind and idea method. Joyce Meyer features a rather tricky expression when describing that. She's got stated that numerous individuals have "stinking thinking."

Everything you choose to consider and reside on within this time of your life may break or make one regarding which kind of man or woman you are going to wind up turning into within this life span.

Leave it to god the father to absolutely catch in a particular one-line sentence by your bible, the trick to becoming in a position to have significant mental wellness inside this living span. After I saw this verse straight back into the old church, it shook off the web page. Right like I watched it, then I watched incredible numbers of sin supporting it

Many Christians haven't heard of the verse as it's straight back in the old testament from the book of proverbs. This powerful verse ought to be memorized with Christians, so because it's supplying us a significant spiritual mystery in having the ability to build an excellent mental health in god.

Here's that the brand-new king James edition of all this poetry:

"As he believes within his heart is, he" (proverbs 23:7)

The essential thing in this verse would be that the phrase" thinks." the phrase" believes" is telling you the god is concentrating on your idea approach -- precisely what you think of daily.

Interpretation -- you are exactly what you believe! You may eventually become precisely what you imagine!

This theory is wildly accepted within our world now. You may genuinely tell who's correctly working with this fundamental principle at how god has planned for us to utilize this who is not.

Even the men and women who always appear to be happy, optimistic, and satisfied with their lives are those that have a fantastic stable mind and that who are generally enthusiastic about and living to the positive matters within their particular life span.

They pick, using their very own completely free wills, to live to the positive side with the daily life as vs. Always believing and residence to the negative side with this life span.

The men and women who aren't joyful and fulfilled, and also who all are at all times cynical and unhappy all of the moment, and also possess adverse attitudes toward anything and anybody, 're about choosing to consider and live on the destructive facet of lifespan.

Allowed this cursed and dropped globe in that all of us are now living within comes with an assortment of life and death within it. Jesus himself said we would have to experience many kinds of trials and tribulations in our life every once in a while.

But, there's a flip side for the coin. However, on the one facet of this scam would be that the darker aspect with this entire life, yet around the opposite point of the currency, would be your sweet, favorable, and also more glowing side with the lifetime. It's perhaps not all passing, despair, and jealousy. In the worst-case scenario and scenarios, there's an expectation and a light at the close of the storm blur tube.

As Christians, most of us possess god almighty himself on our side to aid us in choosing on almost any storm clouds that may come our way inside this living.

The difference between people in life is in their ideal life. Those who are happy at all times, optimistic and positive choose to check to the brighter side of matters, actually in sure of the worse scenario scenarios conceivable.

The unwanted kind of individuals has selected to believe and live on each the terrible things which may happen or make a mistake in such a life span. Irrespective of what good could come to their manner, they are going to feel that anything much better might came their way consistently. Because of this unwanted and harmful form of believing inside their idea process, nothing at all makes them content or happy as nothing else is good enough to these.

The bible is telling us in the verse mentioned above that individuals can all choose things to consider and live on.

We don't need to turn into donors favorable and adverse type believing. To put it differently, we can opt to consider that which you need to find!

Our believing and idea procedure do not restrain us. We restrain!

Damaging type believing could be damaged into

Quite a few, it has grown into a genuine mental strong-hold as they've now been mired into such a negative believing for this a lengthy length of time.

Chapter fourteen

Bring harmony and adoration

Guidelines to bring and maintain love-in your own daily life

Everybody desires to be adored. These tips will help out by bringing romance and love in your life. Utilizing this historical art science and form, it is easy to trigger the adore industry of one's residence to bring and maintain love if you are now solitary or within a relationship.

However, it is likely to come across true romance; even unconditional adore! Listed below are seven measures to locating truelove:

1. Love calls for you to reveal you are true self to a different

The well-known writer, C.S. Lewis, places it most useful, to love at all is to become exposed. Enjoy anything, and your heart is going to be wrung and possibly damaged. In the event you ought to earn sure of keeping it intact, you must give it for no person " Lewis is ideal. Why is love very hard, and at times debilitating, could be that the vulnerability which consistently appears to follow it?

"authentic love goes past the fire of love and possibly locating a mate for that interest to be wed.

We make us of the term wants to spell out a-lot of matters. We adore meals. We adore tunes. We like a good laugh, plus also we love using a sweet moment. Utilizing like to spell out such straightforward matters creates the sentence seem somewhat milder. It's safe as we're not vulnerable. Even a cup of java can't deny us. A tune out of our favorite group doesn't abandon us sense unworthy. However, as soon as we opt to share with you our own life with somebody else, we necessarily earn an option to turn into susceptible. Regrettably,

2. Uncovering true adore can be complicated

The bible includes an excellent narrative regarding a woman called Leah, who detected finding real romance had been not intricate. Leah has been the girl of the manipulative and wealthy man named Laban. Leah had a sister called Rachel, among the absolute most gorgeous ladies in the full location. Leah was clarified as "feeble from the uterus we often do not understand what that term suggests; however, it's somewhat easy to imagine.

Despite the unwanted contrast with her husband, Leah wasn't drawing attention.

3. Your demand for real love shows you should be loved unconditionally

Leah's lifestyle has been filled with the expectation that she might somehow create herself adorably. She had been distressed to locate a means to bring in her spouse's interest. Her busted spirit and despair to be adored educate us that a profoundly particular truth on our search for authentic love. We all have that the devastating weight of attempting to get it done.

Advertisers promote the idea that should be we were a bit more captivating, only a little thinner, more and also a little higher dressed then somebody could finally enjoy note, and we'd feel adored. However, now we do not. Culture disturbs us to place our prudish hesitation and as an alternative giveaway our bodies; additionally, it assures us closeness contributes to like. However, it does not.

"Frankly speaking, authentic love has not been found around passion or romance in the slightest. It's all about value and truth. It's all about acceptance and vulnerability."

4. Truelove is intricate by our self-interest

Allow me to tell you things you probably know but is not always willing to accept. Unconditional love, the type that brings significance and value in your own life, is challenging to discover in still another individual is due to the fact people have been too overly fearful and overly fearful. Our hubs have been bent towards guarding and encouraging ourselves. It isn't difficult to find! We are living in a world that always measures just about every relationship by that which we move free from this. We keep wed just so long because it's profiting us.

We dedicate ourselves to some relationship only until something better will come together. The benefit of the links would be quantified by our demand for adore currently being satisfied rather than looking to fill with the need for authentic love others.

The bible speaks plainly with the actuality. It requires that we are bent towards self-interest sin, plus it had been the manner human kind, nor even the globe was made from the beginning. Adam and eve would be the very first ever to see love; also, it had been substantially darker compared to that which people predict romance now. Adam and eve's relationship have been woven with just one yet, together with god, along with the joy of production round them. There was not any self-interest. As an alternative, their lives had been formed by looking after one another and looking after your world over them and thanking god for your adventure. Neither Adam nor Eve at any time believed an instant of panic, rejection, or even collapse.

"you'll never experience or find precisely the true adoration you are searching for on the planet"

5. There is certainly just one supply of real love

Why don't we come back to Leah's narrative to get a moment? Leah was captured up at the fight to generate her spouse's love-affair. About three sons, later on, she had been clinging to the expectation which specific day he'd awaken and commence to love her. She maintained waiting. Finally, Leah had some other kid, her fourth. Leah telephoned him, Judah, and introduced, "I will commend god." Judah's title indicates something exclusive. This method to commend or be more grateful for god. However, just how can she support god if her external plight had never been changed? Jacob failed to dash house using a bouquet of roses as well as an apology card. Leah is not further admired today than she'd been. However, she had been currently urinating and thanking god.

Together with the arrival of her son, Leah needed a life-changing understanding. She recognized that if her spouse denied to enjoy her, then god was within her entire life! God experienced detected every annoyance, every sorrow, each instant of rejection she'd experienced, and also, he had been massaging blessing to her whole life. God adored her!

6. Accepting Jesus' appreciate opens the door to a new existence

The fantastic news of what Jesus has performed for your maybe not merely salvation out of forthcoming apocalyptic devastation, however, necessitating Jesus' appreciate, will quickly alter and fulfill your life purpose, potency, and enjoy. Much like Leah, you are going to be astonished in the recognition you've detected authentic love! You may flourish from the remarkable enjoyment of worshipping him, having a joyous and pristine soul no matter what exactly is happening close to you.

Your price, along with your individuality, is more procured for all lifetime with Jesus, that loves you passionately that he gave his very life. After you realize that real truth, it alters the direction that you imagine concerning appreciation. No longer will be appreciated exclusively by a romantic relationship that fulfills your desperate desire to detect value and significance. You can approach every new relationship, knowing fully well one's importance. Residing in god's love and after him puts you able of energy that you understand, to whom you belong and that you really might be. You don't need to demonstrate your self-worth or worth. God is yours, and you also really are.

7. Your look for real love starts with this easy prayer

Your true travel love and also to be liked unconditionally starts having a sincere prayer. Could you ever read and imagine that prayer along with me??

"God, now I am visiting profound hurt and rejection. I recognize I have put in my own life seeking value and love inside the incorrect sites. I don't desire to go on living like that. Forgive me for attempting to locate my strategy. Forgive me neglecting you. I remind one even before I know this; you're demonstrating your passion for me personally in Jesus' departure. I am thanking you. His passing delivers me an easy method to learn you and also to have your love. God, fill my heart with a feeling of one's love. Allow me to realize that you're the way to obtain the values and worth. I am hoping you with my own life along with my heart. Cure it allow me to you personally and tease you. Amen."

Appreciate doing his thing

The thought was immortalized in proverbs, music and also the full request of this romantic, "if you like me, then show me," there is something emotionally stunning regarding being advised you might be loved, however maybe not visiting some other signs. But love has been voiced; it needs to proceed outside of words to be contemplated true. It is terrific to possess the voice, way too, however, if that is all there is yes, it's is insufficient.

Appreciate in-action has unique modes of expression

Various varieties of adoring locate distinct manners of saying. Lovers have no profound admiration for expressions that stay inside of the limits of the harmless, determined, appreciative of the young child to have a mother or father. Fraternal adore voiced using an enthusiastic eroticism of the buff could be considered exceptionally improper. Expressions of protecting, civic love in just a peer-reviewed life love relationship looks over-bearing as well as gallop.

It is insufficient to just say how we feel. We have to say the most suitable type of love correctly. Just then does the person adored feel this love moves beyond only words along with the emotional desires of this opposite.

Adore could cloak selfishness

That reminds me that expressions of love could be quite a disguise for selfishness. We typically correlate adore with selflessness and sacrifice, but sometimes careers of love are not anything more than thinly veiled efforts to receive a person's demands achieved. This form of self-improvement usually devolves to expressions of admiration couched regarding endearment. Thus "I like you" only implies "many thanks" and maybe not "I devote you myself." in addition to the human appreciation is entirely passive, so based upon the opposite to start. We might create some telltale signs in emotions of love, nevertheless make it if there's maybe not just a stable positive reaction.

The bible and love-in motion

The bible features a ton to mention regarding really like. Additionally, it recognizes numerous types of person love by the sensual into the charitable, however also the best passages coping with-love would be such that surpass person love and also signed with the celestial. God's love is exceptional as it's untainted by self-improvement motives. It's pure at its saying and unsurpassed in its strength.

Paul wrote, "God shows his love towards us, even when we are sinners, Christ died for people " [romans 5:8] nobody may assert with adore so absolute it goes to departure. All of us can be sure there isn't any hidden agenda, no urge to work out. We may likewise make sure it is unfeigned, for who'd perish for pretense or only to impress?

God enjoys us

God enjoys it because it's his character. He loves to be adored. It's the saying of that he's. We, on the opposite hands, have all to profit by his maxim of love, but for Jesus didn't die simply because of his buddies however because of his enemies, but maybe not just for your pure and sacred, but also the defiled and wicked.

If it comes to appreciate, there is a universe of gap between your type of self-centered, primarily passive adore all folks are utilized to and also the self-giving favorable really as god needs for people.

Chapter fifteen

Be the best version of yourself

Healing crystals you need to attract love and boost your mood

It's 2018, and now we are all aware that crystals are the newest cupid. Rather than waiting for cupid to throw away his arrow take things into your hands and also invest on those crystals to start the center to simply get the love. As stated by crystal healing, diamonds might be utilized to start your own heart to uncover adore and draw a considerable additional.

Every kind of crystal its own healing power, but the most crystals are either be either pink or green! Employing crystals helps in love, relationships, and therapeutic. All these crystals may be used for the majority of types of connections from family to romantic associates and emphasize one of the most significant kinds of appreciation; self-explanatory.

Pink tourmaline

The pink tourmaline rock brings with it plenty happiness and love. It's famous for supporting emotional therapeutic and assists foster disposition.

The way to use: pink tourmaline might be worn as jewelry.

Green jade

Even the green jade stone brings stability in all elements of love and life. The green jade helps bring love and suitable relationships since it brings balance to the chakra of the heart.

The best way to use: you can use it as a necklace. Allow it to break in your own coronary heart.

Amazonite

The amazonite stone is each partners' answer! This crystal assists in conveying improved, the introductory distance for communicating to become more explicit, a lot more receptive & above all, adoring!

The way to use: amazonite could be used as jewelry.

Rose quartz

Referred to as rock of heterosexual, rose quartz might aid with opening your center and curing some previous heart-aches. Rose quartz aids boost inner calmness and self-explanatory that will assist you in ready for your spirit to get fresh like.

The best way to use: you can place it together with your bed or use it. A pendant allows it to break the center.

Green aventurine

Known as the rock of love and fortune, green aventurine enriches assurance and aids espouse shift. Green aventurine helps with full confidence that improves your chance and inspires one to entice fresh, really likes.

The way to make the ideal edition of your-self

Only appear. Assuming you desire to conduct a marathon, however, haven't any prior expertise. The very first rung on the ladder would be picking you up personally shoes and hitting on the sidewalk. Even when you ensure it is a mile in your own very first training jog, you're going to be around 2% closer to a final goal compared if you failed to devote just about any job in the slightest.

2. Start from the beginning. That you never only chance to stumble upon the very optimal/optimally edition on your own. You want to start from the start and require a large number of modest actions as a way to become precisely what you picture eventually.

3. Realize the optimal/optimally variant of yourself ought to become your eyesight, perhaps not anyone else. Do not waste time and energy trying to stay up to precisely what somebody else needs one to be.

4. Quit searching for a critical trick. That isn't any awesome short-cut into this top model of the.

5. Make twitter into the community. It has never been easier to get in contact with

powerful and powerful men and women. Earlier in the day in my profession, I realized a high-tech govt of the business I had been curious about. He had been hosting an am session on twitter. He questioned him to get information about ways to prepare because of his companion, and maybe not merely did he answer some invaluable hints; also, he joined me personally with special men and women in the corporation concerning an open location.

6. Do not sweat the particulars. Just be certain that you're going the right overall leadership. You likely do not have the required data needed to be aware of the shortest road for your own happiness five decades out of now. However, you possibly have any notion about ways to proceed around in the most suitable route. Just take those ways.

7. Acknowledge the chance available. The net has fundamentally changed everything. Formerly, comprehension has been locked out from the minds of sector pros and at the types of novels that you have to get or check out in the library. Now, however, it is easier than ever before to find new expertise. That is critical to turning out to be the optimal/optimally edition on your own.

8. Compose on moderate. Translating your ideas in composed narratives pushes one to consider the thoughts on the mind to a significant deeper degree.

9. Tend not to count those hours. First, they are not an issue. Consider the previous time you conducted onto the treadmill. In the event you looked at the timer just about every few moments, you possibly failed to relish your operation. Then, it left it a lot harder to execute away.

However, what should you choose as a reverse tactic? You plugged into your music player, lost yourself at your new music, also required it you stride at some moment.... While resisting any temptation to take a look in the timer in the slightest. In the event you did this, then you most likely heard you simply enjoyed the series also forced it rather much. Counting hrs. Only slows you down by attaining your objective.

10. Accept help from people. Do not let your pride to be a barrier. Many influential people had assistance across the way, way too.

11. Establish a private internet site. Preserving an internet existence of your-self compels one to turn into the most excellent achievable edition of you personally.

12. Write replies on Quora. Quora can be a very effective assistance which motivate people.

13. Blow off the societal website's scoreboard. People today portray a very exaggerated model of a lifetime on Facebook, Instagram, snap chat, and also other societal programs. We just talk about the fantastic items, but perhaps not just the awful. Therefore, once you assess to which you watch social networking, you are only hurting yourself.

14. Rejoice the little wins. Appreciating everything you are doing at today's grants you the enthusiasm to maintain making strides in the direction of the final objective.

15. stop pretending to understand things you do not understand. You will not ever find such a thing in the event you fabricate to know what.

16. Embrace collapse. Now you cannot come to be the optimal/optimally edition on your own by merely enjoying it secure. But becoming fired may be the optimal/optimally thing which happened for you, only consider Noah khagan (worker thirty in face-book).

17. Telephone your family. That is only the right action to-do. However, you might even learn courses from the family which are not available by way of almost any google hunt and are not available to nearly someone else on the planet.

18. Exercise early in the morning. Once I began doing so in the early hours, I had been a lot more relaxed and concentrated throughout the daytime. Science exhibits up that, as well.

19. Produce a negative undertaking. Doing things such as workout, will helps you to be

happy, enables you to turn into a much better model of the. Thus, whichever it's. A program, album, film, anything. Start carrying it out upon your weekends and nights. And that knows? It may just become a fulltime job which you just simply love.

20. Help different men and women be the optimal/optimally edition of these. Purchase attention ahead. Doing, therefore, stay motivated all on your path, and you might discover the long-term relationships you assemble from aiding the others may substantially help you dancing.

21. Establish your MVP early. In case you do not meet by the present variant on your own, and the fastest approach to fix the problem will always be to start doing work in the direction of the best variant now. That was not any "correct time" to start.

It may be inviting to consider that the optimal/optimally edition of yourself because of a few particular purposes later on. You understand the one where you're:

More effective

Doing exactly what you adore

Existing within a general fitter individual

You view your present personal self because of the standard period, and you are only waiting for those playoffs to commence before committing it all.

What does it mean to turn into the optimal/optimally edition of yourself?

Defining the optimal/optimally edition of your-self

To get started establishing your very best self, then truly have a conversation with yourself only like you had to possess about a very first day. Pretend your perfect person is sitting down with you, and get this man or woman: exactly what activities would you like? Who would you like to reach out to? What impact would you like to make on earth? What is your happiest memory? Be honest and sincere in your answers.

Since you keep this dialogue, cover awareness of someone's feelings. In the event you experience "damaging" emotions such as anxiety or anger, then you are almost certainly telling yourself subtle unwanted messages which vague your dialogue. Delve deeper into what is forcing the atmosphere. Have you been fearful you are going to neglect at discovering? Are you afraid of everything you will see once you dig deep? As tempting as it's always to feel insufficient truly, the reality is the fact that each one people are still fully entire only how we are. It is truly turning into contact with this specific critical self, which may spare one to turn into the optimal/optimally edition of yourself.

The way to turn into the optimal/optimally edition of your-self

As soon as you realize the person you want to be, you will be able to approach the way to turn into the optimal/optimally edition of yourself. Focus on the ending in mind -- your perfect person -- and also require certain things to do to arrive.

Be eager to lose your precious individuality.

If you decide to find your perfect self, you are radically increasing the pub to the men and women that you realize. Your "old self" will withstand this thanks to emotions of bitterness and anxiety about this mysterious. Fight the need to cling to the most recognizable -- that the individuality that is holding back you and adopt a caked mindset.

Tame your fears.

Stress is an insidious adversary that disturbs us both our body and mind and also frees us away out of your present second. Taming your anxieties have its benefits; even so, it is essential to enhance yourself. Once you truly feel stressed, establish exactly what you are scared of and produce down it. After that, jot another excuse, which is not as frightening while being more realistic. Even in case, your emotions do not change straight away, the mind may enroll your justification. With period, the procedure for fact-checking your nervousness gets habitual, and also you become swayed with anxiety.

Prioritize results.

Ever since knowing the way to function as ideal variant of yourself necessitates searching patiently to get intellect, do not decide to wind up by adhering to lots of advice. Permit your perfect person to establish an objective. Pick something possible and ugly, such as becoming reading or organized more information. Building a quantifiable aim is just one of the best techniques to escape from one's head and assemble trust.

Establish reasonable targets.

Prevent mind-boggling yourself from putting tiny, quantifiable objective. In case you want to get rid of 10 lbs., and raise your earnings by 30 percent, then divide down those to smaller measures, such as exercising 20 minutes every time and joining a firm course. Whenever you choose to step towards your aim, you assemble self-confidence to turn into the optimal/optimally edition of yourself.

Conclusion

Since you understand the way to behave as an optimal edition of yourself, you are going to hit roadblocks of fatigue whereby your present set of skills is not insufficient. Do not get frustrated! Amplify your strengths so that you remember that which you are attracted to the dining table. By remaining convinced, you are going to discover resourceful remedies you would overlook if needed stayed calmed down into self-defeating contemplating.

Section of knowing the way to function as a better version of yourself is by learning to work as your boss using effective self-management. Dominant time direction sets you complimentary of stress, steers you in your perfect self-love, and alleviates you of others' anticipations. To remain answerable and in charge of the tools, check-in your progress monthly throughout the year. Turning into your best manager provides you with a much higher resource on the individual team.

www.ingramcontent.com/pod-product-compliance
Lightning Source LLC
Chambersburg PA
CBHW030608220526
45463CB00004B/1210